CLASSIC MARQUES

The tonibell Story

STEVE TILLYER

NOSTALGIA ROAD

First published by Crécy Publishing Ltd 2011

© Text: Nostalgia Road 2011
© Photographs: As credited

All rights reserved. No part of this book may be reproduced or transmitted in any form or by any means electronic or mechanical, including photocopying, recording or by any information storage without permission from the Publisher in writing. All enquiries should be directed to the Publisher.

A CIP record for this book is available from the British Library

ISBN 9 781908 34703 9

Printed in Malta by Melita Press

Crécy Publishing Limited
1a Ringway Trading Estate
Shadowmoss Road
Manchester M22 5LH

www.crecy.co.uk

Front Cover: tonibell depot manager Ray Gibson with his Cummins 'Direct Drive' van in the early 1970s. *Ray Gibson*

Rear Cover Top: Children queue for free Tonis 'Silver Cup' Ice Cream on the Mill Hill estate in north London during the Queen's Coronation of 1953. *George Le-Gresley*
Bottom: A superbly restored example of the van similar to the one pictured on the front cover. This vehicle forms part of the Whitby Heritage Collection in Crewe. *Whitby-Morrison*

Contents Page: Tonis Cream Ices slogan was 'Wins every favour!' — a fitting slogan for quality dairy ice cream that won many awards over the years, including a prestigious Silver Cup. When Tonis rebranded to tonibell the rich recipe was retained and meant that tonibell was soon to became the only national soft ice cream brand to sell a premium 'dairy' product as standard. *George Le-Gresley*

All the illustrations, unless otherwise indicated, are from the author's collection.

DEDICATION

This book is dedicated to my friend and publisher — Alan Earnshaw. Without Alan, two important mobiling stories would not have been told. His enthusiasm and encouragement energised authors such as myself and he is sadly missed. This book was originally commissioned by Alan who sadly died before it could be completed.

Alan is pictured here on the right with me at a *Mister Softee* book signing back in the year 2000.

CONTENTS

DEDICATION	2
FOREWORD	4
INTRODUCTION	5
THE EARLY YEARS	6
THE BLUE YEARS	14
THE PINK YEARS	26
THE OPPOSITION	34
MOBILING: PAST AND PRESENT	48
ACKNOWLEDGEMENTS	63
INDEX	64

Foreword

Everyone, I'm sure, has enjoyed an ice cream from a van at some time in their life. Ice cream is a fun food and the gaily-painted vans are really a part of everyone's life. The ice cream van is a true British icon and an important part of our cultural history. Even in today's high tech way of life, the sound of those musical chimes and a delicious freshly made soft ice cream is still guaranteed to bring a smile to everyone's face.

Mr. Whippy has become the generic term for a soft ice cream dispensed from a machine and, of course, everyone remembers Mister Softee, but the tonibell story is an equally important part of ice cream history. The evolution of tonibell as a brand and the competition between the big three is fascinating. With its rich 'dairy' ice cream, brightly liveried vans and the unique model cow on the roof — tonibell did it their way!

My earliest van memories are from the mid-1960s, when I was pleased to accompany my Dad to the annual ice cream conferences. In 1978, after training as an Engineer with Rolls Royce Motor Cars, I joined the family business. From my weekends working with Dad, I already had a considerable knowledge of the vans and, although I didn't appreciate it at that time, my destiny was to set out to produce the very best ice cream vans. Today, as Managing Director of Whitby-Morrison, I'm proud to work with an amazing group of skilled craftsmen, all with that same passion to produce the very best. The vans themselves have evolved of course and if an original tonibell driver could see a new van working today, they'd be amazed — today's vans are certainly a sophisticated bespoke build.

Despite the importance of continuous development we have not forgotten our past. As an acknowledgement to those pioneering mobilers and to ensure their story is never forgotten, we have assembled a collection of over 50 vans from all ages. In time we hope to have the Whitby-Morrison Heritage Collection on permanent public display and, yes, a bright pink tonibell van, complete with its famous trademark cow on the roof, will take pride of place!

Stuart Whitby
Managing Director
Whitby-Morrison
Crewe

Stuart and sister Julie pictured in the 1960s during a nationwide Ice Cream Alliance Road Safety Campaign.
Bryan & Barbara Whitby

Introduction

THIS book is the culmination of many years of research and is the third book I have written on the subject of ice cream 'mobiling'. Originally commissioned by my friend and publisher Professor Alan Earnshaw, this book has now come to fruition through the encouragement and support of Crécy, the new publishers of the 'Nostalgia Road' series of books.

The term 'mobiling' will be unfamiliar to those outside the ice cream trade but it is a word that is used often throughout this book. So let me explain: in the ice cream trade, a street vendor is know as a 'mobiler' and the vehicles used are known as 'mobiles'. So now you know!

In Britain, we take for granted the ubiquitous and brightly painted ice cream vans that most of us have grown up with. However, it's a little known fact that the United Kingdom is more or less 'unique' in the world by having a tradition of creating bespoke coachbuilt ice cream vans. This is a tradition that endures to this very day. This book not only tells the story of the tonibell brand and its competitors, but is also a celebration of this uniquely British tradition.

The soft ice cream mobiling story started across the pond, on the eastern seaboard of the USA, in the mid-1950s and over here, in the UK, just before the start of the swinging 1960s. As Russ Conway topped the charts with *Side Saddle* and the most important British car ever was about to be launched, the ice cream trade was about to get an innovation not seen since the launch of the Wall's 'stop-me-and-buy-one' trikes in the early 1920s.

The year was 1959, Harold Macmillan was Prime Minister, the Mini was ready to be launched and the famous FX4 London taxi had just begun to be seen on the cab ranks of our capital city. At the same time London saw yet another transport revolution when the groundbreaking Routemaster bus entered general service with London Transport. However, to the wide-eyed kids of that time, it was the introduction of another vehicle that captured their attention. For, just like the flute of the Pied Piper, the chimes of Mister Softee and Mr. Whippy started calling children everywhere. The era of soft-serve ice cream had arrived and tonibell was about to play its part!

Steve Tillyer
Laxton, Northamptonshire
2011

5

The Early Years

Unlike Mister Softee in the UK and Mr. Whippy, the tonibell story starts with another brand some years earlier. As Britain entered a new Elizabethan Age, tonibell was soon to emerge from the established Tonis Cream Ices of north London; this was a brand established over a decade before Mister Softee and Mr. Whippy were launched in spring 1959. However, tonibell did not move over to 'soft-serve' ice cream until Softee and Mr. Whippy had proved that the public's demand for the 'new style' ice cream was strong.

Central to our story in these early years, and well before the launch of the tonibell brand, is a man called George Le-Gresley (pronounced Graylee), whose family originated in Jersey in the Channel Islands. As a lad before World War 2, George had his first experience of selling ice cream when he played truant — bunked off school as George says — and worked with an ice cream vendor with a horse-and-cart. George uses the term 'vendor' as the word 'mobiler' had yet to come into general use.

In 1949 he left the army after having had a spell of service in Nigeria as a radio instructor. Not having any idea of what he wanted to do, he eventually drew on his childhood memories of working alongside the ice cream vendor with his horse-and-cart. He started his ice cream career by purchasing an 'Airborne' trailer, which he towed behind an open-top Morris 8, and converting it to sell ice cream. During the winter months he found employment making canopies for the RAF's trainer aircraft, the Chipmunk. It was during this winter period that George bought another trailer that he also converted to sell ice cream. This 'Romac' trailer is illustrated opposite a few years later during the 1953 Coronation Day celebrations in Mill Hill, north London.

It was around this time that George was increasingly unhappy with the quality of the ice cream he was selling on his north London round. In his search for a better quality ice cream supplier, he approached Tonis Cream Ices of Watling Avenue, Burnt Oak, near Edgware in north London. It was here, in 1950, that George met Ron Peters, the man most closely associated with the tonibell brand. Tonis Ice Cream was sold from Tonis Snack Bar and an ice cream parlour on the other side of the road.

Tonis Ice Cream was established in 1937 by Italian-born Toni Pignatelli and his Scottish wife. They had lived in Glasgow for 14 years before moving south in 1939. By the time their son Ronald had joined the family business in 1949, the snack bar had been joined by a brand new state-of-the-art ice cream parlour, called 'Ice Cream Island', famous at the time for its all-stainless steel approach to hygiene. This was a big investment and included a new ice cream manufacturing facility at the rear of the parlour.

THE EARLY YEARS

Above: George Le-Gresley pictured in his 'Romac' trailer in north London in the 1950s selling Tonis ice cream and Panda Pops' ice lollies.

Right: Tonis Silver Cup ice cream is seen being served here at Ice Cream Island by Mrs Pignatelli sometime in the 1950s. Tonis Ice Cream was made at the rear of the ice cream parlour.
Ice Cream Alliance

Left: Situated opposite Burnt Oak Underground station was Tonis Ice Cream Island. In the early 1950s, this ice cream parlour led the way in the stainless steel approach to hygiene. It was a great source of pride to the Pignatelli family.
Ice Cream Alliance

7

The tonibell Story

By 1951 Peters had taken Tonis Ice Cream onto the streets of north London, using a Dot motorcycle trike. It's understood that this was then joined by a converted panel van. George recalls that the ice cream during this period was made by an employee nicknamed 'Donuts', who, according to George, 'made one of the best ice creams around'. This was backed up by various awards, including a coveted Silver Cup.

The early 1950s saw George establish himself in and around the Mill Hill area in north London as a successful ice cream vendor selling Tonis 'Silver Cup' ice cream and Panda Pops' ice-lollies. Later on Ron Peters, who had changed his name from Ronald Pignatelli, installed an extrusion machine for filling catering and family packs with ice cream. This prompted the move away from scooped ice cream to the cutting of 'hard' ice cream packs on George's north London round. By his own admission, George was hungry for success and a workaholic. Post-war rationing was still causing a problem with regard to the purchase of certain raw materials needed for the manufacture of quality ice cream. As a consequence, George had great difficulty in purchasing as much ice cream as he wanted. Not to be thwarted, George's answer to this problem was to 'procure' a source of the rationed ingredients needed to manufacture quality ice cream. Suffice it to say, he then got all the stock he needed to meet his customer demand.

Tonis Cream Ices' first motorised ice cream mobile (c1951/52) was a 'Dot' motorcycle trike, ridden by George Chislet, which was similar in design to the one pictured here from the Whitby Heritage Collection. *Neil Hickson*

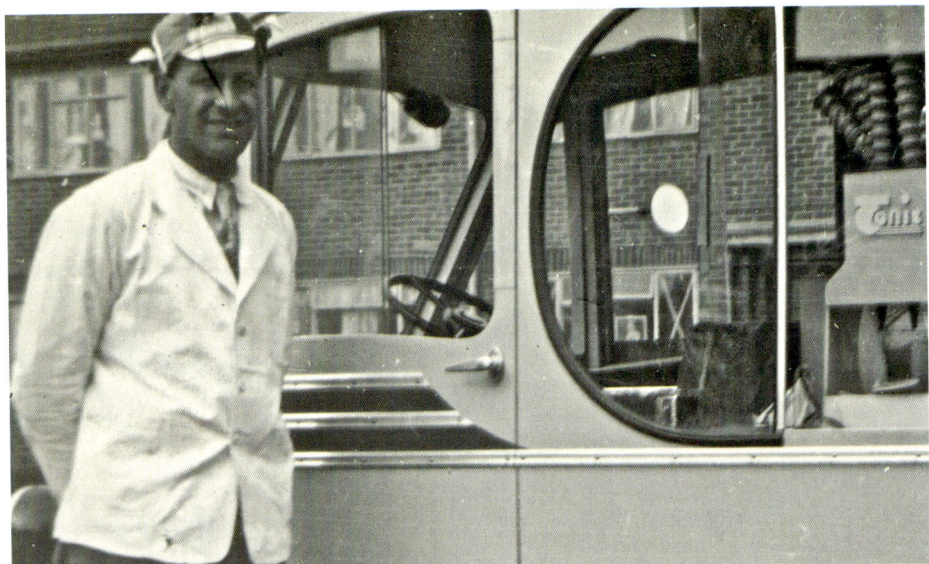

George Le-Gresley pictured beside his first van, a Wadham Stringer-built Morris J type. At £800, this bespoke van was overly expensive but quickly repaid George's investment. *George Le-Gresley*

By 1951 George was totally convinced that 'mobiling' had a bright future and that he was certainly going to be a part of it. So he commissioned a coachbuilt Morris J type — registered FJN 600 — ice cream van from Wadham Stringer of Southend-on-Sea, Essex. This came with a very hefty price tag of around £800. This was an expensive acquisition, being a one-off built to George's exact specifications. However, George recalled that, in those days, he would have to return to re-stock several times a day and his investment was, therefore, soon repaid.

At this time, according to George, Tonis had not purchased any new ice cream vans. George was keen to convince Ron Peters of the merits of his vision for a lucrative 'mobiling' future and that they should work together. According to George, Ron was reluctant at first, so George agreed to purchase another van. This time the services of the Collingwood Carriage Co in north London were enlisted and a price of £600 for a fully-fitted van on the road was soon negotiated. George recalls that it wasn't long before Ron Peters ordered two vans from the same company and the beginnings of the Tonis Cream Ices' fleet had begun.

By 1953 things were going well as a new-found optimism in the country was heralded by a new Elizabethan age and the slow move from post-war austerity to the emergence of a more affluent society. Like most of the country, George and Ron were caught up in the moment and decided to celebrate the Coronation of HM

Queen Elizabeth II by giving away their ice cream on the big day. George managed to obtain some old 'Wall'sie' trikes and cut them down. They were then loaded onto a truck and dropped off at strategic points around his Mill Hill Estate round, along with the Romac trailer and FJN 600. The services of local mothers were enlisted to help serve the children with free ice cream.

This was also a year of expansion with Tonis Silver Cup ice cream now becoming a familiar sight on the streets of north London. The Tonis Silver Cup logo was designed by Ron Peters and proudly advertised the quality of Tonis ice cream on its small fleet of six vans in its now familiar cream and green livery. According to George, it was at this time that he convinced Peters that the way forward was to expand via the franchising route. Drivers were to be encouraged to purchase their vans and, when the drivers had acquired four vans, they would be invited to open a depot in a new and exclusive area.

By 1954 George and Ron had formalised their business relationship by opening the first depot at 1 Bowlers Croft in Basildon Essex. This was under the corporate identity of 'Tonis Cream Ices Basildon Ltd', with Peters holding the controlling interest. George soon moved to Essex to head up this depot and concentrate on

Children queue for free Tonis ice cream on George's Mill Hill Estate round during the Queen's Coronation of 1953.
George Le-Gresley

THE EARLY YEARS

George and Ron enlisted the help of mothers to distribute free Tonis ice cream to children at strategic points around Mill Hill on Coronation Day 1953.
George Le-Gresley

building up the fleet, which at its height was over 20 strong. One of the illustrations in this chapter clearly shows the Tonis Silver Cup logo with the legend 'Wins every favour!'. This soon became a familiar sight in Essex as well as in north London. The Tonis cream and green vans expanded towards the London/Essex borders and George soon opened a further satellite depot in Ipswich.

With the Tonis' fleet growing from an ice cream parlour/snack bar background, it came as no surprise that ice cream parlours started to emerge. These used the Tonis' brand name with London and Basildon having the first ones. It's understood that, when Tonis rebranded, the snack bar/ice cream parlours also followed suit. Today, the tonibell Snack Bar in Borehamwood is the only surviving reminder of this franchised arm of the company.

Back at Burnt Oak, plans were underway to open a new ice cream manufacturing facility and create a home for the expanding north London fleet, which would number 15 vehicles by the following year. With Tonis Cream Ices rapidly expanding, Ron Peters looked for a more modern way to attract its customers. George had used Fulgar-Marshall treble air horns on his van, whilst others used the traditional hand bell or vehicle horn. George also tried unsuccessfully to amplify music on his van by employing an underslung, supposedly all-weather speaker from a World War 2 destroyer. Rain and mud soon put paid to this idea!

In America, some ice cream trucks were already using the forerunner of the ice cream chime in the form of a large and cumbersome unit of tuned metal bars struck by hammers to create a tune. Wall's apparently also used a similar unit to create a chime.

11

The tonibell Story

George Le-Gresley pictured far right (standing) with some of the drivers from his Basildon, Essex, depot prior to Tonis being rebranded as tonibell. *George Le-Gresley*

Although not that common, fire was an ever-present danger in ice cream vans, particularly those with mains generating sets. A fuel leak was the culprit here on this Basildon depot van. Note the now defunct Regent petrol brand in the background and George's American Ford Thunderbird. *George Le-Gresley*

Peters acquired one of these units and approached a company called Harvin and asked if it could develop a smaller and more practical unit. The result was a valve-powered, amplified musical chime. Harvin took a Swiss musical movement — of a type found in music boxes — and fitted a magnetic pick-up that, in turn, was connected to an amplifier and speaker. In 1954, these units were not only heavy, but the valve technology, whilst producing a good sound, drew heavily on the vehicle's battery. By 1958, the modern transistor became available; this immediately alleviated the problem of flat batteries. The transistor dispensed with the need for a power-hungry — and heavy — transformer, which was needed to increase the vehicle's 12 Volts to mains Voltage. The modern ice cream chime was born!

THE EARLY YEARS

By 1955, the plans to open a new factory had come to fruition. Tonis now relocated the whole operation to a new facility on the Barnet by-pass in Borehamwood. This new ice cream manufacturing plant and van depot would also be the head office and hub of the whole operation. The Tonis' fleet continued to expand over the years with new depots being opened on a franchise basis and with the Borehamwood factory supplying all the ice cream and frozen confectionery as well all that the self-employed driver needed on his daily round. The Borehamwood fleet expanded considerably and, in later years, would arguably become the largest ice cream van depot in the country.

Above: The Tonis' fleet was made up of various makes and types of vehicle. Here we see some rebranded Morris J types that were not suitable to be converted to soft-serve vans. *George Le-Gresley*

Right: With an order for 100 new mobiles, confidence was obviously high at Tonis Cream Ices, as the new tonibell brand was about to be launched. At £752 these 'hard' ice cream vans came fully fitted but unpainted from Graham Brothers of Enfield. Vans of this period were a mix of aluminium panels over an ash or hardwood frame, with a good use of GRP panels where more complex shapes were required.

13

The Blue Years

In September 1958 an article in the Ice Cream Alliance journal reported on the forthcoming launch of the American Mister Softee ice cream brand the following year. It's assumed that Peters would have read this article and watched events with great interest. With the public launch of the Mister Softee and Mr. Whippy brands in spring 1959, it's also assumed that he began to formulate a plan in his mind to rebrand and take the expanding franchised operation forward into the 1960s. Another factor at the time was the increasing use, by independent mobilers, both of the Tonis' Cream Ices colour scheme and also of a similar name. Peters saw this as diluting his brand and was probably convinced that rebranding was the way forward.

He, no doubt, looked at the liveries of brands such as Wall's, Lyons, Eldorado and Neilsons, and decided that something different was needed. A new brand image, strong enough to compete and beat the opposition, was the order of the day. During 1959, plans were drawn up to relaunch the Tonis Cream Ices' fleet with a brand new image. Peters commissioned an advertising agency to come up with a brand-new image for the expanding mobile operation. By 1960, this rebranding was well underway and the new all-over blue was a radical departure from the two-tone colour schemes so popular with mobilers at the time. An illuminated pink cow, with a bell round its neck, was placed on the van's roof to become the company's registered trade mark. A brand-new name and the introduction of a unique chime made up the all-new tonibell image.

The company still continued to trade under the Tonis' name until September 1960, when the name changed to the tonibell Manufacturing Co Ltd. Little did the company know that, in a few short years, it would be advertising that it had 'Branches throughout Great Britain'.

Wall's in the 1950s had commissioned the well-known band leader Peter Yorke to create a musical 'call sign' for their vans. The result was the now famous five-note 'stop me and buy one' chime. The American owners of the Mister Softee brand also did the same and created a unique chime for its own trucks. This was then adapted by Harvin for UK Softee vans. tonibell then followed suit with its own distinctive and unique chime, which is still very popular with some mobilers today. Known simply as 'The tonibell chime', it's so far unclear exactly who composed it. It's believed to be the last chime to have been commissioned for an ice cream brand. However, in 1961 Mr. Tasty did create a distinctive 'ding dong' two-note chime, but I'm not sure that this really counts.

THE BLUE YEARS

Posing for the camera in July 1963 is tonibell driver Roger Plummer in his 'ice blue' nylon tonibell coat. The van is a 1960 Graham Brothers-built Bedford CA working out of George Le-Gresley's Basildon depot. *Roger Plummer*

Here we see a proud George Le-Gresley (left) and fellow tonibell franchisee, Bobby White, with some of the Tonis' awards, including the coveted Silver Cup. The picture was taken at the Hendon Hall Hotel during the first tonibell dinner and dance, with Rolf Harris supplying the entertainment. *George Le-Gresley*

The tonibell Story

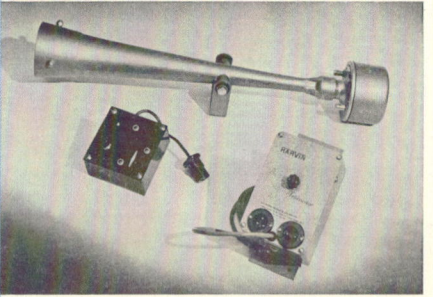

Left: Although Ron Peters did not invent the ice cream chime, it was his request to Harvin in 1954 to develop a modern amplified chime that led to the development of the now famous 'Pied Piper' unit we see pictured here. Initially valve-powered, transistors soon took over from the heavy, power-hungry valve units. *Barry Older (Harvin Chimes)*

Bottom Left: It's said that tonibell was the first to introduce a choc ice on a stick. George Le-Gresley remembers that tonibell, in the early days, was the first company to put in a machine — made by Rose Brothers (Gainsborough) Ltd — to produce a 'choc-ice' on a stick. Rose Brothers built the first automated machine to wrap chocolates, hence the name Roses Chocolates, which is still famous today. Ron Hammond, who worked with tonibell when it joined Lyons, also said that tonibell was also the first to introduce a 'Frozen Yogurt on a stick'.
Borehamwood Museum

16

THE BLUE YEARS

The tonibell chime

*tonibell, tonibell, tonibell time,
tonibell, tonibell, tonibell time,
tonibell, tonibell, tonibell time,
he's around your way,
every day,
at tonibell time'*

The exact date when the name tonibell was thought up is so far unclear, but sometime in 1959 is an educated guess. However, many people at the time would probably not have made the connection between the old and the new name. With Tonis as the old brand and the use of the modern equivalent of the hand bell, 'toni' and 'bell' seems, with hindsight, to have been an obvious choice. This probably prompted the use of the bell round the cow's neck.

The choice of a cow as the company logo and registered trade mark, also underpinned the fact that, unlike Mister Softee and Mr. Whippy, tonibell sold a creamy 'dairy' ice cream, similar in style, to Cornish ice cream.

Few Ice cream companies commissioned their own unique musical chime. In the 1950s Wall's asked dance-band leader Peter Yorke to create a five-note jingle for their 'stop me & buy one' slogan. The American Mister Softee organisation also created a unique tune that is instantly recognisable today. Here we see the sheet music for the specially-composed tonibell chime, which is an instantly recognisable tune and is still a popular choice for today's mobilers. Who composed it and exactly when have yet to come to light.

Opposite bottom right: This trade advert from 1966 extols the virtues of becoming a tonibell driver. This was during the 'Golden Age' of mobiling when the streets were fairly empty and few people had freezers to stock up with cheap supermarket ice cream. Although tonibell drivers worked long and unsociable hours, they were rewarded with an income far above the national average. The handsome driver in the advert is Brian Phillips, whose brother David became tonibell's MD. *Ice Cream Alliance*

Right: Mr. Whippy had a smiley faced cone man with dancing feet and a Tudor bonnet. Mister Softee had 'Cone Head', Eldorado a Polar Bear and Lyons Maid three dancing children as its brand image. It was no mistake that tonibell chose a cow for its brand image due to its rich award winning 'Dairy' ice cream.

17

The tonibell Story

The rise of the tonibell brand to national prominence was recognised by model makers Budgie and later by Spot-on. Today these models can make serious money at auction when in mint condition and, in particular, with their original boxes.

In the heyday of mobiling the handing out of badges to children was seen as a must for all the large mobile ice cream brands. As the Tonis' brand grew through the 1950s and as tonibell into the 1960s, badges were seen as key promotional aids to sales.

With the introduction of the new brand image in 1960, the familiar cream and green Tonis' brand quickly gave way to a strong all-over blue livery. However, at this time, the fleet was still predominantly selling hard ice cream, and Ron Peters was very keen to move over quickly to the 'new style' soft ice cream. The public loved the stuff and Ron Peters knew it, and didn't want to miss a good business opportunity.

George Le-Gresley was busy building up the tonibell fleet in Essex, with a satellite depot in Ipswich in the planning. He was initially very much against converting the fleet over to soft ice cream, but Peters' determination to modernise prevailed. Today, we take for granted that most ice cream vans dispense soft ice cream, but it should be remembered that, in the early days, the cost of an on-board mains generator and a soft ice cream machine was more than the cost of a brand new 'hard' van. This was uppermost in George's mind, as it was with Wall's, a company that was also initially reluctant to invest heavily in the new mobile ice cream technology.

Many of the vans in the fleet were, in fact, unsuitable to be converted to soft-serve and were slowly phased out of the tonibell fleet. The favoured vehicle was the Bedford CA and the standard 15cwt model could cope with the weight penalty of the new equipment — but only just! These vans were sent to Picador, at Sholing in Southampton, for conversion.

When tonibell converted its 'hard' vans to soft-serve, it turned to Onan to power the ice cream machine. Unusually, we see here an ISO counter-top machine in this particular van. This was an early conversion using a machine that was designed for shops and restaurants rather than ice cream vans, along with an LPG-fuelled Onan generator. The ISO was ill-suited to a mobile application and never took off. *George Le-Gresley*

THE BLUE YEARS

This Picador-built van is the shape most closely associated with tonibell in the 1960s. Built on a Bedford CAL chassis, it's one of the longest and heaviest vans built on this particular platform. Unfortunately very few survive today. *Norman Tarling*

Help came in the form of an up-rated long-wheelbase Bedford CA that increased the payload by 2cwt. This in turn allowed Picador to design an all-new — and longer — van for tonibell. For those of us that grew up in the 1960s, it is this shape that we most closely associate with the brand although it now seems clear that it was not exclusively built for tonibell. Period trade adverts seem to indicate that this shape was also available to the trade as a whole and not just tonibell.

At this juncture it's appropriate to take a look at the ice cream itself. It's clear that the new tonibell brand drew on the experience gained over the years with the production of the award-winning Tonis 'Silver Cup' ice cream. However, the new tonibell brand quickly needed to produce a fresh liquid mix suitable for the new soft serve machines that had been introduced on Mister Softee and Mr. Whippy vans in 1959.

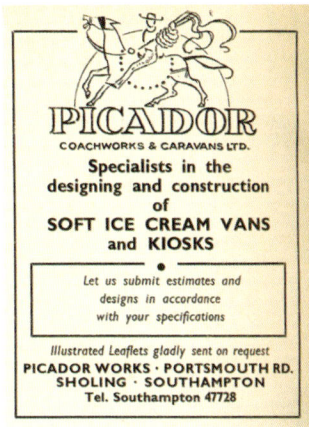

Picador was responsible for converting the tonibell fleet of 'hard' ice cream vans in the very early 1960s to soft-serve mobiles. This obviously gave it the opportunity to convince Ron Peters at tonibell to switch from Graham Brothers to Picador-built vans. *Ice Cream Alliance*

19

The tonibell Story

Here we see an early tonibell van converted to soft-serve, hence the retro-fit roof sticker proclaiming soft ice cream. The Taylor Freeze machine seen here became the machine of preference at tonibell for a number of years and is most closely associated with the brand during its 'blue period'. This was the golden era of mobiling when it was possible to make a living during the winter months. In fact, Ron Peters would often demand that drivers work through even the very worst of the winter weather. *George Le-Gresley*

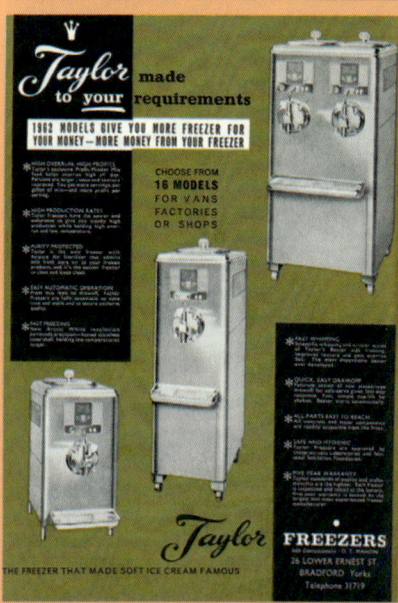

The machine of choice for tonibell vans in the early to mid-1960s was the American-built Taylor Freeze machine. You would be hard pushed to see one working on a van today, although the company is still very much in the ice cream machine business in Michigan, USA. This advert is from 1962. *Ice Cream Alliance*

The fitting of mains generators and soft ice cream machines pushed the 15cwt chassis to its limits. Failed chassis were sometimes encountered as was evidenced by Wall's when experimenting with a Bedford CA. It's fair to say that the Onan generator, with its lightweight construction, made the use of the 15cwt chassis just about viable for soft ice cream vans - that is until 'direct-drive' technology gained the upper hand. *Ice Cream Alliance*

THE BLUE YEARS

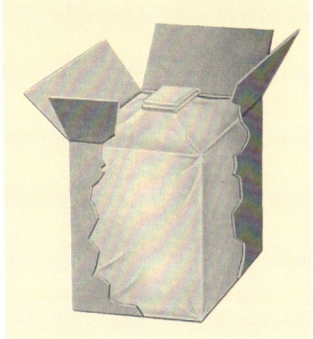

Brands such as Mister Softee produced a standard sterilised mix in US gallon cans that contained non-milk fat. In tonibell's blue years, the factory produced fresh dairy ice cream mix on a daily basis with a very limited shelf life. Pictured here is an Imperial gallon polythene container with a cardboard outer casing. The container pictured here is similar to the ones used by the Borehamwood factory. *Ice Cream Alliance*

This early advert from a local north London newspaper showed that the company had quickly expanded to other parts of the country.
Borehamwood Museum

There had, in fact, been much debate within the industry about the formulation, packaging and storage of the ice cream mix for the new mobile soft-serve machines. By the time tonibell started to convert its vans in 1961, most of the issues had been resolved. However, back in late 1959, the Ice Cream Alliance was also concerned as to whether soft ice cream vans could possibly be forced off the road due to an unsympathetic interpretation of the hygiene regulations. It should be remembered that, in 1959, these vans were regarded as 'mobile ice cream factories', and ice cream factories were required by law to be registered. This fear was further compounded by the mandatory registration of ice cream factory premises, which could include mobile factories. However, this soon proved unfounded and fears subsided.

It's unclear whether the Tonis 'Silver Cup' recipe was modified as the vans moved over to the new mobile soft-serve machines. What is clear, however, are those memories I have of the tonibell product as a teenager and then as a young mobiler in the 1960s. I would often come head-to-head with a tonibell van on my south London round, and the queues at the tonibell van simply said everything.

Unlike Mister Softee and Mr. Whippy, tonibell produced a 'dairy' ice cream that tasted as good as its 'Cornish' cream colour made it look. The public knew the difference but were only able to enjoy its flavour for a short time beyond the Lyons' acquisition of

The tonibell Story

Above: A rare shot of a Picador van in the late 1960s prior to rebranding to 'Hunting Pink' from tonibell blue. By this time most of the vans had lost the plastic red rockets from the upper corners of the rear of the van's bodywork. *Brian Phillips*

Below: Although a very poor photograph, this picture clearly shows the internal layout of the Picador-built vans from the early to mid-1960s. Note the long overhang to the rear of the back axle. The overhang made this particular model the longest Bedford CAL ice cream van in production at that time.

tonibell. Prior to joining the Lyons' family of ice cream brands, tonibell produced all its products at the Borehamwood factory with the liquid mix being made fresh on a daily basis. The mix was packaged in Imperial one-gallon polythene bags and boxed in pairs ready for the van. The mix was then stored in the van's chiller cabinet.

tonibell prospered through the early 1960s with depots initially opening in Basildon, Portsmouth Dunstable, south and east London. The Borehamwood factory was also a van depot and the fleet expanded considerably. From here, the fleet covered a large area of north London and north along the A1 corridor towards the new garden cities.

Throughout most of tonibell's lifetime, the company produced a wide range of frozen confectionery including a few firsts. In the dying years of the brand, it's understood that tonibell packaging was dropped in favour of Lyons Maid branded products. This did not go down too well with die-hard tonibell drivers.

THE BLUE YEARS

This expansion continued at a pace with depots continuing to open throughout England, into Wales and latterly north of the border. Expansion was rapid and it soon became 'tonibell time' on the Stock Exchange in March 1961, the company being the first 'all ice cream company' to be publicly quoted. In summer 1961 Peters entered into negotiations with E. Capocci (Airdrie) Ltd in order to take an 80% interest in this well-known Scottish ice cream company. The idea was to use this acquisition to expand tonibell north of the border quickly. The deal would also see Ernest Capocci join the tonibell Board. This didn't, however, come to fruition, but a deal with Lovells in Wales went ahead to create a Welsh distribution company — tonibell Wales Ltd. The following year Peters tried to purchase a 60% shareholding in the Leeds-based Treats Products. This was not to be, with the Mr. Whippy organisation becoming owners of Treats for just a short period.

Unlike Mr. Whippy, which enjoyed regional ice cream supply, all tonibell ice cream products came direct from the Borehamwood factory. With depots now throughout the country, the logistics of supply and demand became a growing issue, with demand often outstripping supply. George Le-Gresley, from the Basildon depot, recalls that 'at times of peak demand, it was not unusual for me to have to drive to Borehamwood to demand fresh supplies. Keeping my drivers out on the rounds was my first priority'.

Peters had now become a big player in the world of mobiling with tonibell taking its place alongside Mister Softee and Mr. Whippy as one of the three truly national soft ice cream brands to operate nationwide throughout the 1960s and 1970s. Wall's did start to develop a soft ice cream fleet, but its vans were rebranded as Mr. Whippy when Wall's entered into a joint venture with the Mr. Whippy organisation in early 1964.

These companies were now of a size that they began to be to noticed by the City and, therefore, by large companies looking to diversify into other markets. British American Tobacco (BAT) was one of the companies that became interested in tonibell and subsequently entered into negotiations to buy the business. BAT had started a diversification programme in the early 1960s by moving into paper, cosmetics and the food industry. By 1964 a deal was struck and BAT became the new owners of the tonibell brand.

Two Specials with a big future join the Tonibell range at the top end of the price list— Twin Choc Dessert and Strawberry Choc Roll selling at 3/3d. and 3/6d. respectively.

tonibell produced a wide range of frozen confectionery with some directly aimed at the adult market.

The tonibell Story

During the late 1960s, when BAT owned tonibell, the company introduced yogurt. A dedicated sales team was set up to sell to shops and supermarkets.

This was not exactly welcomed by all within the tonibell family, with some franchise holders deciding to leave the brand; these included George Le-Gresley at Basildon, who was now trading as tonibell Essex Ltd. George recalls that this was a difficult time as he and other franchise holders were very unhappy with the deal between BAT and tonibell. It's not clear whether Peters held the controlling interest in all the franchised depots, but the signing of the individual depot contracts was certainly a key factor in order for Peters to close the deal with BAT.

Some four franchise holders left tonibell; these included George Le-Gresley at Basildon as well as depots in Wales and Portsmouth. In fact the Portsmouth franchise holder at Waterlooville opted to go into voluntary liquidation. This depot later emerged as an independent depot being supplied by George Le-Gresley's new ice cream company, Peppis.

With BAT having no experience in the ice cream industry, it relied heavily on the continuity of management at tonibell with Ron Peters remaining with the company until the following year. With BAT's vast experience in marketing to draw on, the public's awareness of the tonibell brand continued to grow. The company now started to market a larger and more varied product range and, in 1966, an extensive

Occasionally authors get it wrong. Identified in our first book — *50 Years of Ice Cream Vehicles* — this mono picture certainly pre-dates the Lyons 'take-over' and is, therefore, not painted in 'Hunting Pink' as previously stated. The window adverts also pre-date the Lyons' takeover and, by the mid-1960s, tonibell had dropped 'Dairy Ice Cream' from its external signage.

building and re-equipping programme began at the Borehamwood factory. BAT was keen to expand into other food related areas and a decision was made to market a yogurt under the tonibell brand. In 1967 the production of yogurt was started and this soon became an increasingly important part of the business. It's thought that later on the first ever frozen yogurt on a stick was introduced.

Little detail is known about BAT's five-year ownership of tonibell and the reasons behind the decision to enter into negotiations with Lyons to sell the company. Today BAT has little knowledge of the company's five-year foray into the world of ice cream mobiling.

The Pink Years

In 1969, negotiations between J. Lyons & Co and BAT came to fruition. For a purchase price of £1,750,000, tonibell Manufacturing Co Ltd now joined the Lyons' family of ice cream brands. These included Lyons Maid and, of course, the flagship Mister Softee brand. It's understood that the purchase was in fact by Glacier Foods Ltd, the wholly-owned J. Lyons' subsidiary that controlled Lyons Maid and its many associated ice-cream activities.

When Lyons bought the company in 1969, tonibell had 22 depots covering England, Wales and Scotland, with parts of the West Country being served from the Salisbury depot. The business, essentially a franchised operation, was credited with operating 500 vans nationwide. Lyons entrusted tonibell's Managing Director, David Philips, with the task of taking tonibell into the 1970s with its all-new brand image. Philips had joined Ron Peters as a driver back in the mid-1950s with his brother Brian joining the company in 1963. Brian recalls that all was not well after the Lyons' takeover and David, therefore, decided to leave the company in 1971 to take over the Borehamwood depot as a franchisee. In addition to the 22 depots, there were said to be 15 ice-cream parlour/snack-bars, many of which were in Greater London and Essex; these were again operated under franchise arrangements. Initially branded as Tonis, they subsequently changed to the tonibell brand.

With the Lyons' takeover in 1969, the production facility at Borehamwood was soon to become a casualty of rationalisation. As tonibell moved into the 1970s with its all new 'Hunting Pink' livery, ice cream production moved to Lyons' Bridge Park factory.

Gone was the fresh 'Dairy' ice cream, in favour of US gallon canned sterile mix. This was very similar (or the same) as Mister Softee and tastee-freez mix. (tastee-freez ice cream was sold in Wimpy Bars.) This change did not go down at all well with the drivers and the public alike, but things soon settled down.

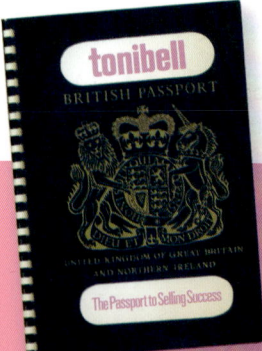

Most of the national ice cream brands — and some regional brands — produced a driver's hand book in order to establish best practice as well as uniformity throughout the fleet. tonibell was no exception as we can see here with this 1970 publication called *Passport to Selling Success*. This 30-page, A4-size book covered everything the driver needed to know, including how to keep the van and equipment in good working order, personal hygiene and the all important consistent time keeping out on the round. *Will Wallis*

THE PINK YEARS

Above: Under the new Lyons' ownership, rebranding produced various attempts to engage and motivate drivers. Here we see a 45rpm record on the front cover of a publication given to drivers by tonibell that featured Managing Director, David Philips, and Marketing Director, John Husband. Some 42 years on, it's interesting to listen to both their 'BBC' style accents.
Tony Connor

Below: In the late 1960s tonibell introduced the Miniball, which could be refilled when returned to the van or shop. However, it has been said that the health authorities subsequently took a dim view of this on hygiene grounds and it was withdrawn from the range.

Tonibell is taking on a new look. Re-styled and distinctive in bright pink. Tonibell vans look different. Are different. They carry a new range of Tonibell products, superbly re-packaged, powerfully backed by sales promotion and display advertising. Tonibell's new marketing policy means business. Tonibell pink is hunting pink. Come in for the kill and share the profits with the pink 'uns.

For information about exclusive franchise territories, write to:
TONIBELL, DEPT. H., FEDERAL HOUSE
2 DOWN PLACE, LONDON W.6

Above: tonibell entered the 1970s with not only a new owner, but also a brand-new striking pink image. However, it does seem rather strange that, in this advert, it chose to use a line drawing of a Budgie model tonibell van from nearly 10 years earlier. *Ice Cream Alliance*

27

This picture shows the last known survivor of one of the static sites and, as you can see, it still retained its original signage. This tonibell snack bar was in Shenley Road, Borehamwood. There were said to 15 tonibell snack bars, with this one being run by Mrs Rita Milone (and her son) who purchased the business in 1969 from Luigi Obertelli, the original franchise holder. Unfortunately it has just recently closed down.

Below Left: When Lyons purchased tonibell in 1969 its plan was to increase the number of depots on a franchise basis. This 1973 map shows that the number of depots had increased little over the first three years of Lyons' ownership. Although tonibell did not actively try to export the brand overseas, it is thought that there were some vans working in Belgium. It's also believed that vans made it to other countries, such as Malta and Australia. *Ice Cream Alliance*

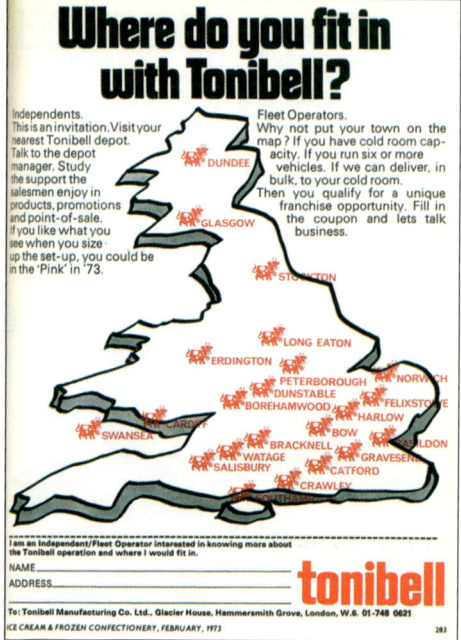

With tonibell production rationalised within Lyons, the Borehamwood factory was now taken over by Bertorelli, with David Philips continuing to run a tonibell fleet from the same site. Bertorelli was Lyons' luxury ice cream brand and was mainly sold in hotels and restaurants.

Notwithstanding the move away from the tonibell trademark style of 'dairy' ice cream, the rebranding, with its bright all-over pink livery, was generally well received and quickly nicknamed 'Kinky Pink' by the drivers. Lyons continued to develop the brand with its own distinctive tonibell products, packaging and point-of-sale material.

In the very early 1970s there was little evidence that the healthy market conditions would not continue. The optimism at Lyons' mobiling franchise division was, therefore, fairly high. New tonibell vans continued to join the fleet, with vans built by Cummins and Morrison now a common site in tonibell's bright pink livery.

THE PINK YEARS

Below: This rather poor quality picture sees Jack Regan (played by John Thaw) from *The Sweeney* getting served at a tonibell — Morrison half cowl — van in the 1970s.

Above: Ice cream vans often made it into the movies. tonibell were no exception and here we see Richard Briers being chased by the 'baddies' in a 1964 Cummins-built tonibell van. This 1972 British slapstick film comedy was called *Rentadick*, which was written by John Cleese and Graham Chapman and produced by the Rank Organisation. It's now available on DVD.

With the patented Cummins 'Direct Drive' system, tonibell had, for some years, been able to dispense with expensive generating sets and, therefore, the heavy 240 Volt electric motor inside the ice cream machine. Morrison of Southampton also produced a direct-drive system. The evergreen Bedford was still much in favour with Ford's Transit continuing to increase in popularity. The Transit slowly moved towards being the favoured chassis for ice cream coachwork as the Bedford had been during the previous decades.

As the tonibell brand moved out of the 1970s and into the 1980s, the writing was on the wall, with the golden years of mobiling slowly becoming just a memory. In 1970, when Iceland opened its first store, less than 5% of the population had freezers but, by 1980, this figure had grown to around 50%. Every mobiler was now not only competing with cheap

An 'drink-on-a-stick' was always a firm favourite from any ice cream van and tonibell was no different in offering its own versions. *Will Wallis*

29

The tonibell Story

Left: This fresh faced 'tonigirl' certainly had big hair and a lot of badges in 1970. *Will Wallis*

Below: The fitting of 'tonibellisima' window stickers with cut-outs allowed flexibility with regard to product and price changes.

Bottom: Like Mister Softee and Mr. Whippy, tonibell offered a full range of products from its vans. This window sticker is from the late period of Lyons' ownership.

THE PINK YEARS

Top Left: tonibell driver Will Wallis is seen here pulling some cones from a Carpigiani machine in 1970. tonibell had, by this time, mainly moved away from the American Taylor Freeze in favour of this Italian machine. *Will Wallis*

Top Right: This Morrison 'Electrofreeze' Bedford CF1, dating from the early to mid-1970s, is fitted with a half-cowl body that utilised the bottom half of a standard CF van body. By this time Morrison Industries had copied the patented 'Whitby' direct drive system and, as would be expected from Morrison, it was a well-engineered copy. However, it's understood that no royalties ever made their way up to Crewe. *Ron Hammond*

Above Right: Most brands used trailers for static site sales such as the one pictured here. However, the Treats' flags indicate that this picture was taken after the demise of the tonibell brand. *Kevin Jennings*

products from the supermarkets, but also the ever-expanding range of corner shops and convenience stores, all of which stocked a wide range of frozen confectionery. These two factors became key in the decline of the mobile ice cream trade.

The continuing story of tonibell is now inextricably linked with the fate of the other Lyons' ice cream brands. The story is covered in the potted history of the Mister Softee brand later in this book and, therefore, does not need to be repeated here. Suffice it to say that morale at the company's mobiling franchise division at Glacier House, Hammersmith, slowly started to suffer. As the 1980s came to a close, it seemed to many that no-one cared. It's understood that it was the same for all of the four mobile ice cream brands that the company owned.

As the 1980s drew to a close the franchised mobiling operation was all but finished. With the Lyons' ice cream division now just a small part of the Allied-Lyons

31

This pretty 'Electrofreeze' van was constructed from many individual GRP panels and almost certainly did not start its life as a tonibell van. It is pictured here after tonibell's demise. *Kevin Jennings*

conglomerate, the future did not look at all good. Effectively our tonibell story ends here, as the brand was all but dead. In early 1992 Clarke Foods bought out Lyons Maid in the hope of saving the Lyons' ice cream brands. This was not to be, as Clarke went into receivership, after a massive rebranding operation, within a staggering seven months. However, Nestlé rode in — like a knight on a white charger — and bought the assets from the receivers. The new owners did, in fact, save the jobs of some 300 employees previously axed by Clarke.

After much consultation, Nestlé decided that mobiling would form part of its future ice cream sales strategy. Having also purchased the Lyons' portfolio of brands, including tonibell, the company had various brand choices. However, tonibell was not to be resurrected. Instead, the Lyons Maid and Mister Softee brands were soon to be seen together on the same vans. This then gave way to an all-new and now more familiar Nestlé Livery.

Was this the end of tonibell? Well, not quite! Now owned by Nestlé, the tonibell brand effectively died when Allied-Lyons sold out to Clarke Foods. But some tonibell vans, owned by franchise holders, continued to trade under the tonibell name for quite some time. Today, one company in Hertfordshire is still trading under the tonibell name as did the tonibell snack-bar in Borehamwood until recently. It's also not unusual to see modern ice cream vans sporting this famous old brand's livery.

The tonibell brand is currently best represented by the beautifully restored Cummins of Crewe Bedford CA, featured on our rear cover. This van forms part of the Whitby Heritage Collection of classic ice cream vans in Crewe and can be hired for special events. For information about Whitby-Morrison, go to www.whitbymorrison.com

It's a serious question.

Every time you get ready to leave the depot you should look at your van from the customer's point of view.

Look inside and out and then ask yourself if you'd be happy to buy from it if you or your family were customers.

A new Tonibell van is the most distinctive ice cream van on the road. Everything about it has been designed to create the most favourable image for Tonibell in the customers' eyes.

Look after your van and you look after that image. Keep it clean. Touch up scratches and scrapes. Stow everything in its proper place. Your van is a reflection of you.

Would you buy from your van?

Is the point-of-sale peeling or appealing?

When did it last see a wash leather?

Does it look appetising?

Is it free from scuffs and dents?

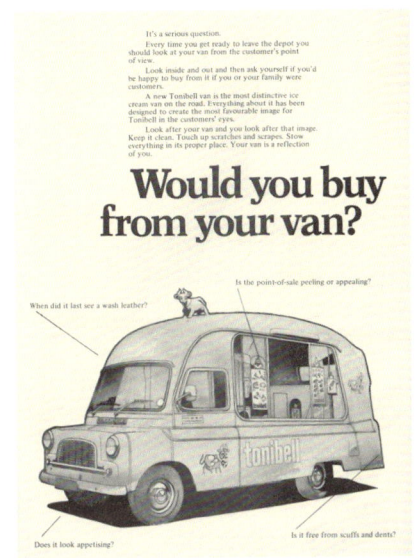

Right: Picador-built tonibell vans were still very much in evidence throughout the 1970s and, as such, were used in the drivers' handbook to good effect as we can see here. Unfortunately, the high standards laid down by Head Office in the handbook were not always upheld, with some depots far worse than others. *Will Wallis*

Below: This 'Hunting Pink' Mark 3 Ford Transit, fitted with a Mark 21 Cummins body, has an original tonibell cow from the 1960s fitted to the roof. Today, this van regularly works a round in Kent and, as you would expect, it also uses the tonibell chimes. *Gary Rich*

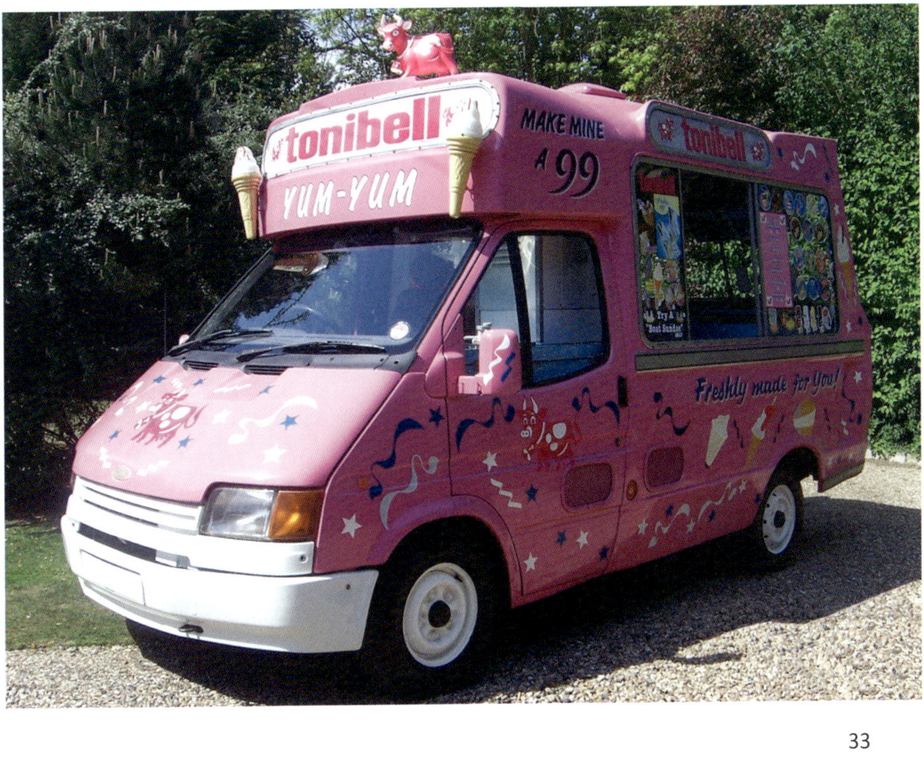

The Opposition

When considering the number of ice cream vans on Britain's streets in the 1960s and 1970s, it should be remembered that independents probably outnumbered the combined size of the national brands. As such they play no less of an important part within the history of UK mobiling.

However, the multitude of small, medium and large regional brands cannot all be represented here in these pages but will, I hope, be a subject for a further book in the 'Nostalgia Road' series. The brands that are represented simply give you, the reader, a taste of this uniquely British tradition.

Mister Softee in the UK

During the autumn of 1958, Britain's very first 'mobile ice cream factory', resplendent in the new blue and white livery of the American Mister Softee organisation, left the factory of Smith's Delivery Vehicles Ltd (SDVL), Gateshead, *en route* to the Commercial Motor Show, Earl's Court, London. What was about to happen next would impact on the trade and change the face of mobiling, in a similar way to the introduction of Wall's 'Stop Me And Buy One' tricycles did way back in 1922.

Left: The iconic 'Cone Head' was first seen in Britain in late 1958 when the American Mister Softee brand was undergoing trials in north-west London prior to the brand's launch in spring 1959. Today, 'Cone Head' is still very much alive and well on the Eastern Seaboard of America.

Opposite Top: Small mobilers have always collectively outnumbered the national brands, but have often been overlooked in the role they played in the UK's mobiling history. Here we see Tina Cox's van that was purchased new in 1962 for £1,900 from Di Di Mascio of Coventry. It's never been restored and can occasionally still be seen on the streets of Leicester. It is the only known Bedford CA surviving today that has exactly the same equipment that was fitted to the Picador-built tonibell vans. Its original Taylor Freeze machine, powered by an Onan generator, still works well some 50 years on. Tina, who has now retired from mobiling, takes great pride in keeping her van in excellent working order. *Phil Consadine*

Opposite Bottom: Mister Softee makes its first public outing at the 1958 Commercial Motor Show at Earl's Court. Twenty of these prototype vans were built; these were initially more expensive than a four-bedroom detached house in one of London's smarter suburbs. *Peter Leeds*

34

Fresco Kreams
Cox's
Fresco Kreams
BEDFORD
540 DRY

Mister Softee
Mister Softee

The tonibell Story

SDVL had secured the UK Mister Softee franchise in order to bolster its production of coachbuilt vehicles. However, it was not seriously interested in moving into the mainstream ice cream business and, therefore, approached J. Lyons & Co, Cadby Hall, London.

The initial contact was to see if Lyons would be prepared to make the ice cream mix for SDVL to the American Mister Softee recipe. However, it soon became clear to Lyons that SDVL was not just looking for a supplier of ice cream mix, but also a business partner. Initially sceptical, this gave way and the Lyons' board eventually sanctioned a joint venture company with Smith's. In January 1959 Mister Softee Ltd was formed — jointly owned by SDVL and Lyons — with SDVL holding the controlling share.

Mister Softee vans soon started to roll off the production line and, by April of that year, franchise holders in Kent, Essex, Greater London and the Midlands were taking delivery of their new vans. The first batch of 15 vans quickly grew to a hundred by the summer of 1960. Mister Softee had now entered the 'Swinging '60s' with a bang and a new era of prosperity for mobilers had begun. Sadly it was not to last!

The initial cost of the first — twin-machined — vans was prohibitively high at £3,200, but SDVL quickly developed a new specification with a much lower price tag of £2,300. By the start of the summer of 1961, Mister Softee had established 34 locations in England and one in Wales. Mister Softee was now beginning to take off in a big way and Lyons knew it had a winner on its hands. As the brand continued to expand throughout the early 1960s, Lyons looked to take full control of the joint-venture company. It decided to make SDVL a substantial offer for the latter's majority share-holding in Mister Softee, which after some haggling, was accepted in the middle of the decade.

This picture was taken in summer 1959 shortly after the launch of this, the first 'Soft-serve' mobile ice cream brand in Britain. The public took to soft ice cream in a big way and mobiling was about to change forever.

36

THE OPPOSITION

This 1967 van was built by 'Electrofreeze' of Southampton, by then part of Morrison Industries Ltd. The van has a fairly complex body made from many individual GRP panels including the bonnet and scuttle. Built on the Bedford CA chassis, the body was then fitted to Morrison's own patented 'Powerdrive' chassis utilising Ford running gear. *Tony Connor*

This then brought the whole Mister Softee operation under the umbrella of Glacier Foods Ltd, a wholly-owned subsidiary of Lyons.

By the mid-1960s it was patently clear that the cost and size of a Softee van were no longer required. Bryan Whitby of Crewe had already developed the 'Direct Drive' system, which, in effect, eventually killed off the use of generators. However, Mister Softee continued with generators for a while but now fitted to the smaller Bedford vans produced by Morrison Electrofreeze of Southampton.

The Mister Softee franchise operation, although continuing to grow throughout the 1960s, had started to slow by the time Lyons — through Glacier Foods — acquired tonibell from BAT in 1969. As the new decade dawned, Mister Softee, although by now a household name, had peaked. Competition in the mobile sector was now intense, more and more houses had deep freezers and, therefore, purchased ice cream from the fast-expanding supermarket chains, which offered cheaper take-home packs. Every corner shop offered a full range of ice cream products, as suburban streets, although not yet totally congested, were filling rapidly as the British became more affluent. The writing was on the wall…!

The tonibell Story

Fast forward to the 1980s, and the Lyons' ice cream franchise division started to take its eye off the ball as mobiling in general was entering into a period of decline, with little hope of recovery. It seemed that no-one cared at head office any more and, to many, it appeared that Mister Softee and the other Lyons' brands had been left to fend for themselves.

By the end of the 1980s, the franchise operation was all but finished. With the lack of attention, the mobiling sector within Glacier Foods seemed to lose its identity and became absorbed into the mainstream business of Lyons Maid, itself just a small part of the giant conglomerate Allied-Lyons.

This 1961 Mister Softee Karrier once belonged to the author and has now been fully restored by classic ice cream van enthusiast, Gary Sutton. The van no longer has its generator and Sweden Freeze machine, but dispenses ice cream from a period Italian machine powered from the van's modern diesel engine.

THE OPPOSITION

Below: When Nestlé purchased the Lyons Maid family of ice cream brands from Clarke Foods, the new corporate name became Nestlé-Lyons Maid. In time this gave way to Nestlé branding alone, with names such as Mister Softee and tonibell being consigned to history.

Above: In the decade since the first ever book on mobiling was published by Nostalgia Road, interest in classic ice cream vans has grown considerably. As such, many more vans destined for the scrapyard have now been saved for posterity by a new breed of enthusiasts. Two such enthusiasts are Keith and Fred Metcalfe of Tamworth, who have helped keep the Mister Softee name alive by restoring two 1960s Commer Softee vans. Pictured here after winning some serious silverware, they were shocked that a commercial vehicle could win 'Best in Show'. No mean feat when you consider the fantastic classic cars they were up against. *Keith Metcalfe*

In 1991 Allied-Lyons took the decision to sell its family of ice cream brands including Mister Softee. Early in 1992 Lyons Maid had a new owner: Clarke Foods. Amid fanfares and theatrical relaunches Clarke Foods was heralded as the saviour of Lyons Maid — but how little we knew! Cracks in the business immediately appeared and, by September 1992, Clarke Foods was in receivership — and all in just a matter of seven months. Like the 1966 World Cup many people 'thought it was all over' — but it wasn't! A knight in shining armour came riding over the hill in the form of Nestlé, the Swiss food giant.

Nestlé bought the assets from the receivers in November 1992 and, by so doing, saved about 300 of the jobs axed by Clarke. So began the rebirth of a British institution, but with a slight name change: Lyons Maid, a name as familiar as Rolls Royce, had risen from the ashes as Nestlé-Lyons Maid.

Mister Softee as a brand in the UK was now defunct with the new Nestlé-liveried vans only acknowledging Mister Softee in the form of a small vinyl sticker. Today, a handful of the early Mister Softee vans have been lovingly restored and are now safe in preservation for future generations to enjoy.

39

Mr. Whippy

In 1958 an Anglo-Italian entrepreneur, Dominic Facchino, visited the USA and was taken with the new Mister Softee concept of mobile ice cream factories as they were sometimes called back then. The impact of these 'trucks' on Dominic was such that he immediately entered into negotiations with the Irish-American Conway brothers, who owned the brand, in an effort to secure the Mister Softee franchise in the UK. As we have seen in the previous section, the UK franchise went to the more established Smith's Delivery Vehicles Ltd.

Undeterred, Dominic returned home to the UK secure in the knowledge that mobile soft ice cream had immense potential. He quickly set about formulating plans to establish his own mobile soft ice cream brand. By late 1958 the Mr. Whippy concept was formulated. Dominic gave up his lucrative £5,000-a-year job with Nielsons, the Canadian ice cream company, and formed a £100 company based in Leamington Spa. Joining him on the payroll were his two sisters along with his trusted nephew, Peter Hopkins, who also gave up a well-paid job to join the embryonic Mr. Whippy team.

It was decided that the best way forward was to set up a pilot scheme of six vans in Birmingham and monitor the public's response to the 'new ice cream factories on wheels'. A similar scheme in London was soon to follow. Although confidence in the Mr. Whippy concept was high, it was nevertheless a big gamble when considering that initially five 'hard' ice cream vans could be purchased for the cost of one Mr. Whippy van at £3,400. However, like Mister Softee, the high cost would soon be dramatically reduced.

A livery of pink and cream was chosen to be distinct to that of Mister Softee, which had one of blue and white. The now familiar chime, based on *Greensleeves*, was adopted along with a smiling faced Mr. Whippy man logo, which survives today as one of the most iconic ice cream brand trademarks. The Mr. Whippy man wore a Henry VIII style bonnet and was given 'dancing feet', the end result being an instantly identifiable brand image to rival the American Softee 'Cone Head' trademark.

Anglo-Italian entrepreneur Dominic Facchino launched the Mr. Whippy brand just a matter of weeks after the launch of Mister Softee and, in doing so, created the now famous Mr. Whippy man so instantly recognised even today. The name Mr. Whippy has now slipped quietly into the English language as the meaning for an ice cream served directly from a machine.

The first vans were introduced in Birmingham during April 1959, just a few weeks after the UK launch of Mister Softee. A new company — Mr. Whippy Ltd — was formed on 1 April 1959 and a sister operation of six Mr. Whippy vans soon followed in Hounslow, west London, run by Ernest Pacitto, a business associate of Dominic's.

Pacitto, who was already operating vans under the Mylo's brand in west London and Southend-on-Sea, also produced the ice cream mix for the Mr. Whippy pilot scheme in London. He was also the UK agent for Carpigiani of Bologna, a manufacturer of soft ice cream machines. It was Ernest Pacitto who convinced Carpigiani to develop a van model of its twin-barrelled freezer. This move proved to be a key element in the operational success of Mr. Whippy and also established the reputation of this Italian manufacturer as a leader in mobile soft-serve machines.

Lyons was just ahead of the game with its involvement in the launch of Mister Softee a month earlier. However, Dominic's fear was that players, such as Wall's, would respond and, therefore, squeeze him out before he could get up and running. Fortunately for Dominic, Wall's demonstrated an apparent total disinterest in soft ice cream mobiling. It's fair to say that this was quite common at the time, as many in the trade were extremely sceptical about the future of soft ice cream mobiling and said that it was just a fad, due to its high capital and maintenance costs. Mr. Whippy, Mister Softee and tonibell were about to prove them all wrong!

From the outset, the rapid growth of Mr. Whippy was achieved through franchising the operation. However, the emerging profitability of fleet operations meant that the business would continue to grow on two fronts, with company-owned vehicle numbers just exceeding the franchised operators by the end of the third year of trading.

The Mr. Whippy organisation continued its rapid growth during 1961, with company and franchised depots opening at quite a pace. They soon linked up with the substantial Northern Dairies, which produced Mr. Whippy ice cream mix and ran a fleet of 50 Whippy vans. Northern Dairies soon took a 'substantial' interest in the Mr. Whippy organisation.

An Ice Cream Alliance article in spring 1961 states that 150 Mr Whippy vans were on the road with another 175 in the pipeline. However, by August 1962, Mr. Whippy company figures state that there were 800 vehicles in operation nationwide. This published figure does seem a touch on the high side and it's suspected to be part of the age old tradition of 'advertisers puff'. Whatever the exact figures were, one thing was for certain, Mr. Whippy had now come of age and was emerging as a household name — a brand that subsequently became strong enough to slip silently into the English language.

The Mr. Whippy brand was now established as a truly national player and surely one that the 'big boys' could no longer ignore. Enter Charles Forte, who Dominic knew from his visits to the Café Royal Sporting Club in London. Dominic had obviously whetted Mr Forte's appetite during their informal chats at the club and, as a consequence, it was decided to enter into serious negotiations for the Forte Group to acquire the Mr. Whippy organisation. This proved successful and overnight made Dominic Facchino the newest member of the millionaire club.

At this point there were 735 Mr. Whippy vans on the road, with 374 owned and operated from company depots. There were 23 company depots operated by various companies in the group and 56 depots run by franchised agents. I think it was fair to say that as 1962 came to a close, there was no doubt that Mr. Whippy ice cream could be bought in every densely populated area of England and Wales, with strong inroads being made in Scotland. This was also the year that saw the Whippy brand leave our shores for sunnier climes, but that's another story.

As Mr. Whippy entered 1963 as an integral part of the Forte empire, there seemed to be little day-to-day evidence of change. The Forte broom had obviously not felt the need to sweep clean and clearly demonstrated the faith that Charles Forte had put in Dominic Facchino and his team. Facchino remained as Chairman and Managing Director, with a lucrative seven-year contract, and Peter Hopkins continued as General Manager.

On paper the deal looked good: Mr. Whippy had demonstrated a healthy profitability in the previous two years, but all was not as it seemed. Charles Forte would

Here we see the only surviving van from the Mr. Whippy fleet that has seen continuous use from the 1960s and is still working today. Long-term owner, Howard Mitchell, still maintains the van to its original specification with the original machine and generator still in good working order. Howard and his van can be seen during the summer months at the Trumpington Garden Centre near Cambridge during most weekends.

soon learn that all was not rosy in the Whippy garden, as trading losses soon became evident. In fact, losses would soon amount to £500,000.

The company may have been losing serious money but, to the drivers and franchise holders, this was the heyday of soft ice cream mobiling and sales by today's standards were extremely high with vans often getting through 30 gallons of mix each day.

During the summer of 1963 Charles Forte and Wall's started negotiations, as the latter had clearly missed the boat with regard to its own involvement with soft ice cream mobiling and was keen to regain lost ground. Although Wall's was already running a limited number of soft ice cream vans, the company had failed to react to the early success and subsequent rapid growth of the Mister Softee, Mr. Whippy and tonibell brands.

Of the larger fleet operators, only tonibell made the wholesale transition to soft serve ice cream. Wall's, therefore, saw in Mr. Whippy an opportunity not only quickly to catch up, but also the chance to eliminate a competitor in a market sector that it now needed to take more seriously. By the end of summer 1963, an agreement had been reached and a joint venture company would soon merge the Wall's mobiling operation with Mr. Whippy. This arrangement would later be known as Wall's-Whippy Ltd, a partnership of equals, with management and financial control jointly shared between Wall's and Forte.

The next two years saw a great deal of change and, after the initial chaos of amalgamation, a new optimism began to grow as the rationalisation and integration of the two fleets and depots became a workable reality. On the franchise front, new agents were continuing to join the brand in encouraging numbers and it soon became clear that the emphasis of Wall's-Whippy would have to move in the direction of a wholly franchised operation.

At the end of 1963, prior to amalgamation, Wall's direct selling fleet consisted of 147 soft ice cream vans, 499 wrapped vans and 363 of the smaller 'minivans' such as the left-hand-drive Ford Thames 7cwt. Of these, 611 operated under the new Wall's-Whippy company for the 1964 season. Some vans from the Wall's fleet were deemed to be too old to join the new combined fleet! When the full amalgamation of the Mr. Whippy and Wall's mobiling fleets was complete, it was estimated that an 1,800-strong mixed fleet made it the largest in the country. Of these, about 1,000 would be selling soft ice cream, branded in Mr. Whippy colours, whilst the remainder continued in the traditional blue and cream Wall's livery.

Whilst Mr. Whippy continued to make good profits for drivers and franchised depots, Wall's-Whippy Ltd as a whole was far less fortunate. By the end of summer 1964, a loss of £400,000 was recorded. In 1966 Wall's purchased Forte's shareholding in Wall's-Whippy Ltd. Now fully under Wall's control, the Mr. Whippy brand would enter a new era, where company-owned depots continued to decline in a gradual move towards a fully-franchised network of depots running both Wall's and Whippy

Here we see another 1960s' Mr. Whippy van badged as a Karrier. It was recently returned to its former glory by Dave Cummings & Sons of Tyneside, who were at pains to reproduce the correct shade of pink and cream as used on the very early vans. For a period it worked for a living with owner Ian Smith of Leeds but it has recently been sold to the Whitby Heritage Collection in Crewe. *Ian Smith*

vans. By 1968 the whole Wall's-Whippy operation had become fully franchised and Wall's began to see positive results from its investment and restructuring programme.

Anecdotal evidence suggests that, in the better years that followed, the nationwide network of franchised dealers rose to around 100 whilst the combined Wall's-Whippy fleet numbers fell to around 1,000 vehicles. Unfortunately, a detailed history of Mr. Whippy after Wall's fully acquired the brand in 1966 remains a mystery. Today Mr. Whippy is still an independent and a well-known brand in Australia and New Zealand.

Mr. Whippy as a distinct brand in the UK continued through the 1970s, with many vans still liveried in Mr. Whippy pink and cream through into the 1990s. However, the main thrust for Wall's became the promotion of the core Wall's brand with Mr. Whippy slowly fading away. Several decades on, the exact year that Mr. Whippy officially ceased to be an active Wall's brand is still unknown, even to Wall's!

Today, ice cream mobiling is totally dominated by independent operators. However,

THE OPPOSITION

Many well known names such as Francis Rossi (Status Quo) and Duncan Bannatyne (*Dragon's Den*) have been mobilers in their youth. Here we see a van owned by Rupert Grint of Harry Potter fame. A fan of ice cream vans, Rupert chose the Mr. Whippy theme for his restoration of this Morrison Electrofreeze CF. Note the non-original three-colour scheme that really suits the Electrofreeze bodywork. *Courtesy of* Classic Van & Pick-up *magazine*

Wall's and Nestlé have both continued to promote their brands through the tried and tested franchise route. This has enabled both companies to keep their brands highly visible to the public, through distinct branding, up and down the country.

Mr. Tasty

In early 1961 plans were made to launch a new brand of soft ice cream under the name of Mr. Tasty. This London/Essex-based brand will mean nothing to those in other parts of the country. However, if things had worked out differently, Mr. Tasty could well have developed nationally.

At the helm was a Mr A. E. Pelosi, who was also the Managing Director of Perfect Flavour Ice Cream, the east London suppliers to Mr. Whippy. The company began trading in spring 1961 with Pelosi and three other directors. Again the Italian influence was seen in the gaily-coloured Commer vans built by Bonallac & Sons of Basildon in Essex. It's also believed that Bonallac was a partner in the new venture.

The tonibell Story

Mr. Tasty vans were virtually identical in design to the early Mr. Whippy vans built on the Commer/Karrier 30cwt chassis. The pale blue vans with red, white and green stripes, soon started to be seen on the streets of east London, Watford, Dartford and Gravesend, where the company had opened depots.

Pelosi was already supplying fresh liquid mix to Mr. Whippy, through East London Perfect Flavour that was sold to Mr. Whippy in August 1961. Dominic Facchino saw that controlling the supply of ice cream was a key factor in the continued success of his expanding Mr. Whippy operation. However, the relationship with Pelosi must have been very strong indeed, as Pelosi remained in day-to-day charge of the company in spite of the fact that Mr. Tasty was now up and running as a competitor. Pelosi continued in this role when the Mr. Whippy ice cream production moved from east London to a new state-of-the-art factory at Basildon in Essex.

A new innovation at Mr. Tasty was the removal of the normal workload that drivers had at the beginning and end of each working day. Gone were all the cleaning, maintenance and re-stocking chores normal to most mobilers. Pelosi said at the time: 'Mainly the idea is to enable them to spend longer time selling, but the directors believe, too, that salesman can be at their best only if unhampered by unnecessary duties.'

Another novel idea of Pelosi's was to reduce the length of the ice cream chime to simply two notes. This was said to be an attempt to be less annoying to the public. Mind you, it didn't work, as the 'ding-dong' chime was played several times over by the drivers who came down my street in Walthamstow in east London.

Mr. Tasty was conceived as a brand that would in time grow into a major player and, therefore, needed a strong visual image. Here we see a Bonallac-built van in its bright Italian colour scheme. Mr. Tasty's trademark was a young lady kneeling and holding a large cone, with the legend stating 'Italian Maid'. These vans weighed in at well over three tons and had massive TVO-fuelled generators to power the twin Carpigiani ice cream machines.
Ice Cream Alliance

The vans proclaimed 'Always Fresh For You', which was, in fact, quite true as the mix was made fresh daily. I suspect that the Mr. Tasty ice cream mix was similar, if not the same, to that Pelosi was producing on a daily basis for Mr. Whippy at Perfect Flavour and subsequently at the new Basildon factory he went on to manage for Mr. Whippy. Like tonibell, the liquid mix was packed in gallon polythene bags with a reinforcing cardboard outer.

The early vans had an expensive and very heavy Italian twin-barrel, drip-fed Carpigiani ice cream machine. This, along with the freezer and chiller cabinet, was powered by a Ford Consul (12.5 kva) generator producing 415 Volts. These vans were heavy and tipped the scales at well over three tons. These vans were powered by a commercial version of the robust 2,267cc, overhead-valve four-cylinder petrol engine from the Humber Hawk.

Unlike Mister Softee vans, those of Mr. Tasty were virtually indistinguishable in design from the early Mr. Whippy Commers and, therefore, had the same clever features. Drivers enjoyed easy access to the serving area via a swing seat, which permitted a 180-degree clockwise movement and thus no more tripping over the handbrake and gear stick. However, it was a shame the van's ceiling height was only designed for those under 5ft 10in. These vans also had a floor-to-ceiling offside door in the serving area. This was great for washing out each day and loading stock. On a static pitch, the door could be opened and fixed to the rear bodywork. Anyone who has worked one of these vans will tell you how hot they can get in the summer months.

I remember the drivers being colour co-ordinated with their vans. Their three-quarter length coats being in pale blue, the same as the main colour of the vans; the pale blue was also extended to the radiator grill and wheels. Drivers, on leaving the depot, had to look in a mirror alongside a picture of an immaculately dressed salesman. The caption said: 'Do you look like this?' The forage caps didn't stand the test of time and were probably only worn as the drivers were leaving the depot. The company trademark was a kneeling figure holding an oversized cornet and proclaiming 'Italian Maid'.

Like Mr. Whippy and tonibell, the Mr. Tasty brand also expanded into static sites. The first was at David's in Oxlow Lane, Dagenham, which opened in May 1961. The vans at this stage were all owned by the company, but plans for expanding through a franchise scheme were said to be under consideration for the 1962 season.

It's so far not clear as to what extent this brand had expanded and indeed how long they survived in business. With four depots opened by summer 1961, they were certainly expanding, with the Plaistow depot said to be operating an impressive 20 vans. This was evinced when visited by a reporter from the trade press at that time.

In preservation — and now owned by the author — is what is believed to be the last surviving Bonallac-built Commer 30cwt ice cream van. If any reader has further information about this Essex coachbuilder or, indeed, Mr. Tasty (Italian Maid) Ltd, I would much appreciate you making contact at mister.sundae@virgin.net

Mobiling: Past and Present

Although tonibell as a brand did not survive into the 21st century, the name can still be seen on many ice cream vans today. These include a superbly restored Bedford CA, which forms part of the extensive Whitby Heritage Collection in Crewe.

As noted previously, the mobiling sector of the industry went through a period of decline in the latter part of the last century, with many household names, including tonibell, disappearing. In fact, serious investment in the mobiling sector by the large companies had all but finished. tonibell was sold off to the ill-fated Clarke Foods along with all the other Lyons' ice cream brands in 1992 and Wall's was also in the process of killing the Mr. Whippy brand in favour of Wall's-only branding.

The Clarke Foods' takeover of Lyons Maid was a fiasco that left the industry stunned and resulted in questions being asked in the House of Commons, whilst hundreds of jobs hung in the balance. New owners Nestlé took a long hard look at the business and decided that the 'mobiling' sector had a future, but only as a fully franchised operation. The Lyons Maid and Mister Softee brands were sidelined with tonibell being consigned to history along with the Midland Counties brand.

Today, neither Nestlé nor Wall's own fleets of ice cream vans — the economics just don't stack-up. In fact the UK mobiling industry has, for many years, now been made up of individual mobilers and regional operators. However, many of these small operators have bought into the Nestlé or Wall's franchise and, therefore, the image of a national branded fleet has been maintained.

Although national brands such as tonibell, Mister Softee and Mr. Whippy have long gone, some individual mobilers are reluctant to let the names die completely. It is, therefore, not unusual to see these old names kept alive on brand-new vans.

Opposite we can see the van belonging to Gary Rich, who still uses the tonibell name in memory of his Dad who was for many years a tonibell driver. Another old tonibell driver, Will Wallis, still runs tonibell (Southern Counties) Ltd in Hertfordshire and regularly works a round to this day. In fact Will was extremely helpful in bringing this book to fruition.

When this cartoon was drawn some 200 or so years ago, ice cream was virtually the sole preserve of the wealthy. The Victorian era was to see this slowly change as ice cream started to become more widely available and its cost reduced.
Ice Cream Alliance

MOBILING: PAST AND PRESENT

In the period after Nestlé took over Lyons Maid, several ideas were considered, including this 1994 attempt, to stimulate sales on a wider front. The 'filling station' concept, with a wide range of sales items including hot dogs, hot drinks and Nestlé chocolate, did not take off as hoped for. This was probably the last time Nestlé used the Mister Softee and Lyons Maid brands on their vans.

This recent picture shows Gary Rich in his tonibell van. Gary is keeping the tonibell name alive in honour of his Dad who was a tonibell driver for many years.

49

The tonibell Story

Ice cream is generally regarded as one of those products that everyone loves and is certainly taken for granted today, being available everywhere and with more choice than ever. The history of ice cream has been covered in many books before, including earlier volumes in the 'Nostalgia Road' series, so I'm not going to delve into that subject matter here. However, centuries ago, when ice cream was in its infancy, it was certainly the sole preserve of the rich and much favoured by royalty. Anyone knowing the secret of ice cream making would surely have a secure future, with the first recipe reportedly not being published until the 18th century.

Fast forward to the Victorian era when recipes for ice cream had started to become fairly common knowledge and simple ice cream machines had become available. A new market started to open up to those who could afford this frozen treat.

Early ice cream machines consisted of a wooden bucket with a central metal container. Ice and salt were placed in the cavity between the bucket and the metal container that contained the liquid ice cream mixture. This was then turned by hand with a paddle. The simple action of churning the mixture could produce a fairly even full-bodied texture ice cream. However, this resulted in a much heavier product than today's commercial offerings, due to significantly less air being introduced into the freezing process. In fact several small ice cream makers, such as Criterion Ice Cream, boasted that they sold 'solid ice cream — not air' well into the 1950s.

Ice was obviously a key factor in the production of ice cream and, at this point in history, the technology to produce it did not exist. Ice would, therefore, have to be imported by ship from places such as Norway and Canada and then taken by barge up river to specially built ice-houses.

Left: Very early ice cream machines consisted of a metal container within a wooden bucket with ice and salt placed between them. The ice cream mix was placed in the metal container and mixed by hand with a paddle to introduce air into the mix whilst freezing occurred. This simple method could produce a good even-textured ice cream. The picture here shows a much later version, but the principle remained the same.

Opposite: Carlo Gatti was an entrepreneur from the Italian-speaking part of Switzerland. He was to become a key player in the development of ice cream in London during the Victorian era.

Today some of these ice-houses still exist and can be visited by members of the public at the London Canal Museum near London's King's Cross (www.canalmuseum.org.uk). At this time an embryonic ice cream industry was starting to form and it will come as no surprise to learn that it was the Italian community that was in the vanguard of subsequently taking ice cream to the general populace.

The supply of fresh milk was also a key factor in the production of ice cream. Fresh milk supplies to our towns and cities had always been problematic as a result of fluctuating supply and demand and the product going off due to lack of refrigeration. With the availability of ice in places such as London, it became a business opportunity to turn surplus milk into ice cream, rather than pour it down the drain. Initially customers would have to seek out ice cream vendors, but that would change as the ability to conserve ice cream allowed its sale to go 'mobile' — hence the term 'mobiler'. However, this particular term was not used in the trade until a very much later date in the next century.

In the early days, a man called Carlo Gatti, from the Italian-speaking part of Switzerland, became one of the key players in the introduction of ice cream mobiling. He was responsible for creating huge ice pits just north of King's Cross station, which, in turn, helped make the commercial production of ice cream a reality. It's said that Gatti then went on to open a network of cafés and to employ salesmen with barrows and hand carts to sell his freshly made ice cream. However, this embryonic period of mobiling was not the most hygienic of times. Ice cream would often be served in a glass known as a 'Penny Lick' and then handed back to the vendor to serve the next customer. Suffice it to say the glass was not washed first! Concerns over the spread of TB and other diseases meant that this practice was eventually stopped. Grease-proof paper was also used but the later introduction of the ice cream cone, invented by Mrs Marshall, was to become a major step forward, whilst adding another edible product to the fun of eating ice cream.

The start of the 20th century saw the ice cream industry grow throughout the country and many Italian families moved to England, Wales and Scotland to become an integral part of that business. Many Italian immigrants had no knowledge of ice cream making, but soon took to it like a duck takes to water. Italian carpenters and wheelwrights were just a few of those immigrants who turned their hand to ice cream and cone/wafer making as a new trade. Suffice it to say, their old skills became very useful in making the vehicles needed to ply their trade.

The tonibell Story

Penny Lick glasses come in various shapes and sizes, but were all created to dispense ice cream, with the glass then returned to the vendor. This practice was eventually stopped as the glasses were rarely washed between customers. *Courtesy of Leeds Museums & Galleries*

Mrs Marshall became famous for many things including her cooking and ice cream recipes and had several books published on the subject. She is also credited with inventing the edible cone, which in the fullness of time would revolutionise the serving of ice cream by vendors, in 1888. This predates the American claim to the invention of the edible ice cream cone by some 16 years.

It's fair to say that Britain is more or less unique in the world in having a fine history of bespoke coachbuilding of ice cream mobiles. Much of the artistic flair, which can be seen on vans today, can be traced back to those early Italian pioneers — but that's another story for a future publication.

Much is talked about the big players in the history of the UK ice cream industry and rightly so. However, it should also be understood that the independent mobiler — small companies and family concerns — has collectively always made up the majority of the mobile trade in this country. As such, the sector represents a worthy subject matter in its own right and, it is hoped, this will form a future volume in this series.

Over the first two decades of the 20th century, the ice cream industry established itself, but no one had yet produced ice cream on a more industrial scale. Enter T. Wall & Sons, purveyor of meat products to royalty and the subject of an earlier book in the 'Nostalgia' Road series.

Once Wall's had diversified into ice cream and frozen confectionery, the company quickly appreciated the popularity of and, therefore, demand for this frozen delight. This demand was soon to be met after a brand-new Wall's factory was built at Acton in

Above: Whilst this is assumed to be a pre-war photograph, the use of horse-drawn ice cream carts was still evident in some areas well into the 1950s.

Right: Collectively, regional operators made up the larger part of the mobile sector and not the big national fleets. Here we see a consignment of 13 Bedford CAs ready to be delivered to Rossis of Walthamstow, in east London, where the author grew up. *Ice Cream Alliance*

west London. The factory, known as the 'Friary', was soon to develop full scale ice cream production on a more industrial scale, with a cone and wafer factory following later on.

It was at this point in history that one of the most important mobiling innovations took place: the introduction of the 'Stop Me And Buy One' trikes in around 1922. This innovation soon mushroomed to reach every corner of the country with thousands plying their trade by the outbreak of World War 2. Customers would place a blue 'W' in their window to indicate that a call from the 'Wall'sie' man was required.

Wall's was not to be alone in seeing the potential of diversifying into ice cream mobiling. J. Lyons & Co, established in 1887, was developing its food empire and ice cream as a whole was to play its part, although the exact date Lyons started large scale ice cream production seems unclear, as does its entry into company-owned mobiles. In later years Lyons would expand through the acquisition of many famous ice cream brands.

Before World War 2, the use of motorised vehicles for mobiling was not commonplace, although many fine examples of motorised ice cream coachwork had been produced as far back as the Edwardian era. In the 1920s or 1930s you were more likely to see a trike or hand/horse drawn cart than a motorised ice cream van. That said, the building of bespoke ice cream vans was well established before starting to be more commonplace after the war.

Much of the artistic flair associated with ice cream coachwork can be traced back to the very early days when immigrant Italian artisans would paint their ice cream carts with elaborate, bright and colourful designs. Here we see a superbly restored Frederick's of Chesterfield Morris PV, which demonstrates beautifully this artistic legacy.

A Wall's delivery driver stands by his Ford model T van that delivered ice cream from the company's factory at the Friary, Acton, west London. *Birds-Eye Wall's*

MOBILING: PAST AND PRESENT

Thousands of 'Wall'sie' trikes plied their trade on the streets of Britain in the 1920s and 1930s. However, whilst always thought of as a male preserve, this rare picture proves that girl power existed long before the Spice Girls were even born!

After hostilities ended in 1945, severe rationing across the board, not only made raw materials for the production of ice cream difficult to obtain but also new vehicle chasses were as rare as hen's teeth. This was due to the Government's 'Export or Die' campaign as Britain grappled with the crippling debt from a World War.

It was during this period that many pre-war cars and vans were rebodied to accept ice cream coachwork. Unitary methods of car construction had yet to become 'the norm' so small coachbuilders were still commonplace and, therefore, happy to produce one-off coachwork. As the popularity of ice cream vans increased during the 1950s, several coachbuilders started to offer brand new, fully-fitted ice cream vans as part of their vehicle range. As monocoque car construction started to become industry standard, the coachbuilding industry as a whole began to shrink with several companies turning to mobile shop coachwork to help keep their order books healthy.

Eldorado was absorbed into the Lyons' family of ice cream brands, which were later rebranded as Lyons Maid. However, those of you old enough will remember the Eldorado girls during the intermission at the local cinema.

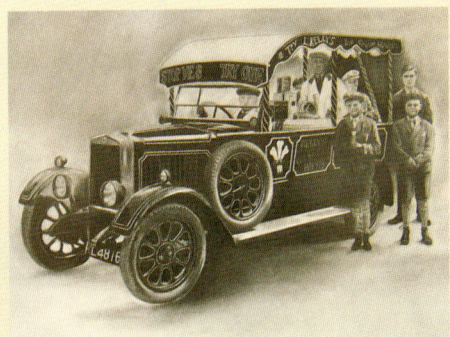

Before World War 2, you were more likely to see a trike or a hand/horse-drawn ice cream cart than a motorised ice cream van. However, many fine examples of motorised ice cream vans have been produced ever since Edwardian times. Here we see a 1925 Morris Cowley of Kelly's Ices with six Kelly brothers posing for the artist. *Phil Kelly*

The tonibell Story

Whilst many coachbuilders were going out of business, others continued by seeking out new markets such as mobile shops. Several firms decided to specialise in this area, including S. C. Cummins of Shavington near Crewe, Archibald Scott of Bellshill in Scotland and Smith's Delivery Vehicles of Gateshead, to name just a few. Cummins is worthy of special note here due to the fact that this company became synonymous with the ice cream trade as part of the mobiling industry, rather than just a supplier to it.

After the introduction of soft ice cream vans in spring 1959, Cummins and others were quick to offer their own 'mobile ice cream factories' as part of their range of vans. However, Cummins was soon to develop — and subsequently patent — a new system for powering the ice cream machine. Mains-powered generating sets were not only heavy and expensive, they generally required a larger, more expensive and, therefore, less manoeuvrable chassis.

Several coachbuilders specialised in 'mobile shop' coachwork with Smith's of Gateshead being one of the bigger players who were looking to increase their market share. Having secured the American Mister Softee franchise around the time this advert was published, Smith's quickly designed an all-new van in order to launch the mobile soft-serve concept to the public in 1959. *Ice Cream Alliance*

In the 1960s Cummins of Crewe became a household name in the mobiling industry, with the 'Whitby' direct-drive system cementing its position. Here we see a trade advert from 1964 showing two of its models. What the advert didn't say was that, for £2,370, you could own your own business without being contracted to any particular brand. A Mr. Whippy Commer at this point would have cost £2,400 with a contract that tied the mobiler into exclusively purchasing from one supplier. *Ice Cream Alliance*

This new system was the brainchild of Bryan Whitby, who had joined Cummins in the early 1950s before leaving in 1962 to start Bryan Whitby Refrigeration in Crewe. The principle was a simple one: harness the power of the van's engine, via belts, shafts and electromagnetic clutches, to power the soft ice cream equipment. This would then allow the use of the smaller and cheaper 15cwt chassis such as the Bedford CA, which was much favoured by mobilers of the time. After the inevitable teething problems, the new system was unveiled to the trade at the Ice Cream Alliance Exhibition at Rothesay in Scotland. As Cummins direct-drive van production got underway for the 1964 season, it's fair to say that Bryan's innovation was set to revolutionise the mobiling industry.

The 'direct-drive' system was patented in 1967 by Bryan Whitby and S. C. Cummins Ltd and today is still the industry standard, being used throughout the world. However, there were several attempts to dispense with conventional generating sets over the years. Several companies tried various innovations including a power take-off from the van's gearbox. This drove a mains voltage alternator that powered the ice cream machine and refrigeration equipment. Another idea was the use of a Velocette motorcycle engine to power the van's equipment. It's believed that this worked via a centrifugal clutch that engaged when the engine's speed was increased. It was apparently rather problematic for various reasons and the idea was not developed further.

The idea of a direct-drive system had in fact already been exhibited at the 1961 Ice Cream Alliance Exhibition in Scarborough by a Birmingham company called Walter Relph Ltd. Research has shed little light on the exact type of system the company was exhibiting, except for its listing as exhibitor number 35, which stated: 'This year the company will be showing a direct-drive ice cream freezer for mobile application and delegates will have the opportunity to inspect the machine on two sales vans equipped with it'. It's not clear at all what 'direct-drive' means in this particular instance, except to say that it's believed that an agricultural type 'donkey' engine was employed to power the van's equipment.

Throughout the immediate post-war period the mobiling sector grew at a fair pace and with the introduction of the 'New Style' ice cream in 1959 that growth accelerated. In retrospect, this was seen by many as the 'golden age' of mobiling, in a period before widespread supermarkets, home freezers and congested streets. By the end of the 1960s, the majority of vans were being produced by a handful of specialist coachbuilders, with soft ice cream vans continuing to increase in market share. When the direct-drive system was introduced, in the mid-1960s, the mobiling sector was still increasing in size, but that was not to last. By the end of the 1970s, a decline in mobile sales had become evident and, by the 1980s, many of the specialist coachbuilders had gone out of business.

As the 20th century came to a close, the mobiling sector had shrunk considerably. Street mobiling was the hardest hit, with most houses now having cheap supermarket frozen confectionery in their home freezer, and congested streets making it much more difficult to 'stop me and buy one'.

The tonibell Story

Although most of the specialist coachbuilders had long gone, the building of bespoke ice cream coachwork is still very much alive and well in the 21st century. In 1989 Whitby Engineering of Crewe purchased — from Robin Hood Engineering — the Morrison name along with the tools and moulds to build the highly respected Morrison Electrofreeze vans that utilised a one-piece Glass-Reinforced Plastic (GRP or fibre-glass) construction. In 1998 Whitby-Morrison as the company was now known, bought out S. C. Cummins Ltd after the latter had completed nearly half a century of producing 'mobile shop' coachwork.

Over the next decade, the influence of Morrison and Cummins was very much in evidence as Whitby-Morrison continued to develop its range of body styles on various chassis and for markets around the world. Ice cream vans have come a long way since the introduction of the first soft ice cream vans in 1959. Today, vans are

This body of this pretty 1964 Bedford CA was designed and built by Cummins and fitted out with an early 'Whitby' direct-drive system by Bryan Whitby Refrigeration in Crewe. This van is identical to the one the author drove on his south London round in the 1960s. These very early direct-drive vans did not have an electromagnetic clutch on the engine in order to disengage the ice cream equipment's drive system whilst driving. As a consequence, they proved very noisy indeed as road speed increased. Another clutch was soon introduced which transformed the driving experience.

MOBILING: PAST AND PRESENT

no longer wood framed, but utilise fully-integrated GRP bodies mated to a chassis/cab of the customer's choice. Today's mobilers can enjoy the creature comforts that the writer did not have when he was a mobiler in the 1960s. Back then, power steering, heaters, stereo and relatively quiet equipment were yet to become commonplace in soft ice cream vans.

So what was it like to be a mobiler back then and also now in the 21st century. Our book here sets out the story of the tonibell brand, so who better to ask than a mobiler who is keeping the tonibell name alive on his round in Kent. Gary Rich now takes up the story:

'Things have changed a great deal from when I was a young boy and was working with my Dad on his tonibell van. In those days we would start our round at noon and carry on through into the late evening. In fact, we

Here we see a 1964 model (blue) Picador van in an empty suburban street in the late 1960s. Today street mobilers can only dream of the relatively empty streets we all enjoyed back then. Note the new external signage introduced around the mid-1960s. Although the rich dairy tonibell recipe was said to have remained unchanged, the vans were now strangely devoid of the word 'Dairy' and indeed 'Ice Cream'.

The tonibell Story

This Kelly's of Barnsley van on a Bedford CF chassis has a Glass Reinforced Plastic (GRP or fibre glass) one-piece body by Morrison-Electrofreeze of Southampton. Morrison's coachbuilding division pioneered the use of one-piece GRP body construction at a time when the use of aluminium panels over a wood frame was still the industry standard.

Today's new ice cream van bodies are built on the experience gained from decades of composite body construction. Today, many old Whitby-Morrison vans are still working for a living long after their normal life expectancy; this is a testament to the longevity of the design. Here we see a current Whitby-Morrison model on a Mercedes chassis, a combination that will set the owner back a cool £60k. A big investment maybe, but 50 years ago a Mr. Whippy van on a Commer chassis at £2,400 would roughly inflate to over £80k in today's prices, if based on the average earning's index. *Whitby-Morrison*

MOBILING: PAST AND PRESENT

Here we see three generations of coachbuilders (and ice cream engineers) outside the Whitby-Morrison factory in Crewe. Far left is the inventor of the 'direct-drive' system, Bryan Whitby, standing next to his son Stuart Whitby, the company's current Managing Director. On the right is Stuart's son Ed Whitby. *Whitby-Morrison*

sometimes finished at 10.30pm, which would be unheard of these days. In those early days we only sold ice cream, but quickly we began selling other products such as sweets, crisps and drinks. In the winter months, we sold almost anything we could, to keep going until the sun came out again.

'It's amazing to think that back then the cost of a soft ice cream van was as much as an average detached three-bedroomed house and I can even remember Dad going out on his round on Christmas Day. My Mum then decided she also wanted a van and Dad knew David Cummins at Crewe. She was soon out driving the first of the Cummins-built Fiat 238 vans. It had a Taylor Freeze machine fitted and was painted bright pink and of course had tonibell chimes.

'Today we still work to tonibell values, as set out in the 1970s mobiler's handbook called the *Passport to Selling Success*. These were given out to all drivers joining the tonibell family. Today, our Ford Transit vans are presented with uniformed, well-trained staff and we are licensed by the local council and proud to be upholding the high standards and rules that have been in place for over 50 years. Living the tonibell theme means our customers can rely on us to be there on time, put a smile on peoples' faces and above all, sell quality products. My Dad would certainly be proud.

The tonibell Story

'It's fair to say that the supermarkets have made a big dent in the viability of all street mobiling, as we simply cannot compete with their prices. However, we still have a loyal following that means a living can still be made if you work hard, keep to your times and sell quality products at a fair price. Other vans have come and gone over the years but we stay constant and are proud of what we do.

'Events and weddings see us at our best as you can't miss our bright pink vans against any backdrop or fun fair stall. Our 'tonibellissima' fans that remember our Teddy Bear, Double Delta and Genie lollies still get a kick out visiting our tonibell vans. Today we still sell strawberry sundaes and fruit cocktail boats as well as many of the favourites that my Dad sold all those years ago.

'Sunshine still plays a big part, as the slightest drop of rain can see profits halve and streets empty. My 15-year-old son now works the streets as I did with my Dad and, of course, he has heard the stories of the old days many times over. In those days it was not unusual to have several vans turn up outside one block of flats. On one occasion, Fresh Whipp, Criterion and Rossi came into a street at the same time. It still puts a smile on my face when I remember the children running to us as they heard the tonibell van coming.

'You can tell from what you have read that I'm passionate about what I do and also keeping the tonibell name alive. This is something, I hope, I have passed onto my son. My dream today would be to drive into Albert Square or a remake of *The Sweeney* with my tonibell chimes ringing out. Sadly I have no pictures of those bygone days with my Dad and his vans. I would ask anyone with any information to get in touch with me through our web-site at www.tonibell99.co.uk.'

Gary Rich.

Like grandfather, like son, like grandson. Three generations of tonibell men in the same family must be a one-off, as the tonibell brand has officially been defunct for many years now. However, 15-year-old Lain Rich, pictured here, is set to keep the tonibell name alive for at least a few more years — in Kent that is! *Gary Rich*

Acknowledgements

This book could not have been written without the help of those listed here. The author is indebted to you all: George Le-Gresley; Brian Phillips; Kevin Jennings; William Wallis; Gerry Ryan; Stuart Whitby; Bryan Whitby; Ed Whitby; Gary Rich; Ray Gibson; Jennie Tillyer; Howard Mitchell; Philip Kelly; Tina Cox; Andy and Bev Ballisat; Kevin and Margaret Donovan; Ron and June Hammond; The Ice Cream Alliance; Harvin Chimes; Barry Older; Robin Weir; Ian Smith; Peter Hopkins; Adrian Bailey; Elstree Borehamwood Museum; The tonibell Café, Borehamwood; Gary Sutton; Tony Connor; Nestlé; Birds-Eye Wall's; Jacqueline Phillips; Phil Consadine; Matthew and Bryony Richardson; Gordon Lack; Leeds Museums & Galleries; Lisa Greene; Jenny and Malcolm Kindell.

Index

Airorne Trailer 6
Allied Lyons 31, 39
Archibold Scott Ltd 53, 56
Bannatyne, Duncan 45
Basildon 12, 15, 23, 24
Bedford 29, 37
Bedford CA 18, 22, 33, 34, 48, 57, 58
Bertorelli 28
Birds-Eye Walls 54
Bonallac & Sons 45, 47
Borehamwood 11, 13, 21, 23, 24, 26, 28, 32
Borehamwood Museum 16
Bowlers Croft 10
Briers, Richard 29
Bryan Whitby Refrigeration 58
Bridge Park 26
British American Tobacco (BAT) 23, 24, 25, 26
Budgie Model 18, 27
Burnt Oak 11
Cadby Hall 36
Capocci 23
Carpigiani 31, 41, 47
Chapman, Graham 29
Chislet, George 29
Choc Ice 16
Clarke Foods 32, 39, 48
Cleese, John 29
Collingwood Carriage Co 9
Commer 39, 47
Commercial Motor Show 34
Conehead 17, 34, 40
Connor, Tony 27, 37
Consadine, Phil 34
Conway Brothers 40
Conway, Russ 5
Coronation 1953 ....9, 11
Cow (tonibell) 14, 17
Cox, Tina 34, 35
Criterion Ice Cream 50, 62
Cummins 28, 29, 33, 56, 57, 58
Cummings, Dave 44, 61
Cummins, David 61
Dancing Children 17
Di Di Mascio 34
Direct Drive 37, 56, 57
Dot Motor Trike 8
Earnshaw, Alan 2, 5
Eldorado 55
Facchino, Dominic 40, 41, 42, 46
Fiat 328 61
Ford Consul 47
Ford Thames 43
Ford Thunderbird 12
Ford Transit 29, 61
Forte, Charles 41, 42, 43
Fredericks of Chesterfield 53, 54
Fresh Whipp 62
Friary, The 53, 54
Fulgar-Marshall 11
FX4 Taxi 5
Glacier Foods Ltd 26, 27, 37, 38
Glacier House 31
Gatti, Carlo 50, 51
Graham Brothers of Enfield 15, 19
Greensleeves 40
Grint, Rupert 45

Hammond, Ron 16, 31
Harris, Rolf 15
Harvin 12, 14, 16
Henry V111 40
Hickson, Neil 8
Hopkins, Peter 40, 42
Humber Hawk 47
Hunting Pink 22, 26, 33
Husband, John 27
Ice Cream Alliance 7, 14, 17, 20, 21, 27, 28, 41, 46, 57, 48
Ice Cream Island 6, 7
Jennings, Kevin 31, 32
Karrier 38, 44
Kelly's Ices 55
Kelly's of Barnsley 60
Kelly, Phil 55
Kinky Pink 28
Le Gresley, George 6, 7, 8, 9, 10, 11, 12, 13, 15, 18, 19, 20, 21, 23, 24
Leeds, Peter 34
Lovells 23
London Canal Museum 51
Lyons 14, 21, 22, 27, 28, 41, 53
Lyons, J & Co 26, 36
Lyons Maid 17, 22, 26, 32, 38, 39, 48, 49, 55
McMillan, Harold 5
Mercedes 60
Metcalfe, Keith & Fred 39
Mill Hill 8, 10, 11
Milone, Rita 28
Mini 5
Mitchell, Howard 42
Mister Softee 5, 6, 14, 17, 19, 21, 26, 30, 31, 34, 36, 38, 39, 41, 43, 48, 49
Morris 6, 8
Morris Cowley 55
Morris J-Type 9, 13
Morris PV 54
Morrison-Electrofreeze 31, 37, 45, 60
Morrisons 28, 29
Mrs Marshall 51, 52
Mr. Tasty 14, 45, 46, 47
Mr. Whippy 5, 6, 14, 17, 19, 21, 23, 30, 40, 41, 42, 46, 47, 48, 56, 60
Mylos 41
Neilsons 14, 40
Nestle 32, 39, 45, 48, 49
Northern Dairies 41
Obertelli 28
Older, Barry 16
Onan 18, 20, 34
Paccilo, Ernest 41
Panda Pops 7, 8
Pelosi 45, 46, 47
Penny Lick 51, 52
Peppis 24
Perfect Flavour 45, 46, 47
Peters, Ron 6, 8, 9, 10, 12, 14, 16, 18, 19, 23, 26
Phillips, David 17, 26, 27, 28
Phillips, Brian 16, 17, 22
Pied Piper 5, 16
Pignatelli 6, 7, 8
Picador 18, 19, 22, 33, 34, 59
Plummer, Roger 15

Polar Bear 17
Queen Elizabeth 10
Regent Petrol 12
Rich, Gary 33, 48, 49, 59, 62
Rich, Lain 62
Robin Hood Engineering 58
Romac Trailer 6, 7, 10
Rose Brothers Ltd 16
Rossi Francis 45
Rossi's 54, 62
Rossis of Walthamstow 53
Routemaster 5
S. C. Cummins Ltd 57, 58
Sheet Music 17
Side Saddle 5
Silver Cup 7, 8, 10, 11, 15, 19, 21
Smith, Ian 44
Smith's Delivery Vehicles Ltd (SDVL) 34, 36, 40, 56
Spot-on 18
Sutton, Gary 38
Sweden Freeze 38
Sweeney The 29
Tarling, Norman 19
Tastee Freeze 26
Taylor Freeze 20, 31, 61
Thaw John 29
Tillyer, Steve 1, 2, 5
Tonibell Chime 17
Tonibell Essex Ltd 24
Tonibell Ltd 21
Tonibell Manufacturing Co Ltd 14
Tonibell Miniball 27
Tonibell Snack Bar 11, 28
Tonibell Wales 23
Tonibell Yogurt 24, 25
Tonibellissima 30, 62
Tonis Snack Bar 6, 9, 10, 11, 12, 14
Tonis Cream Ices 9
Tonis Cream Ices Basildon Ltd 10
Tonys 3, 6, 7, 8
Treats 23, 31
Velocette 57
Walter Relph Ltd 57
Wadham Stringer 9
Wallis, Will 26, 29, 30, 31, 33, 48
Wall's 5, 14, 18, 43, 45, 52
Wall's-Whippy Ltd 43
Walsie Trike 10, 34, 55
Whitby, Bryan 37, 57, 61
Whitby Direct Drive 31, 56
Whitby Engineering 58
Whitby Heritage Collection 8, 33, 44, 48
Whitby-Morrison 60, 61
Whitby, Ed 61
Whitby, Stuart 61
Wimpy Bar 26
White, Bobby 15
Yorke, Peter 14, 17